The Author's AI Toolkit

From Concept to Publication

Hank Quense

License notes

Published in the United States of America.
Published by Strange Worlds Publishing.

Acknowledgements

The cover artist on this book was Gary Tenuta: gvtgrafix@aol.com
Nanci Arvizu and Karin Abarbanel were my beta readers

Table of Contents

Getting started with Artificial Intelligence (AI)

Why Writers & Authors Should Care About Artificial Intelligence.

There's a lot of value to viewing AI as another practical tool in a writer's kitbag. Used effectively, it can:

- Provide wide-ranging research support
- Help jumpstart stalled projects.
- Spark ingenuity and new ideas
- Support creative brainstorming
- Make marketing easier and more fun.

The key to harnessing AI and making it work for you is learning how to frame queries — how to target requests so AI can help you with planning, unleash your creativity, and enrich your book projects in exciting ways.

That's what this book is all about. By the time you finish reading it, you'll know what a useful, practical tool AI can be for developing every phase of your book project from planning through marketing. You'll also have plenty of examples of actual AI queries to inspire you and simple techniques you can use to get maximum value from your own tailored AI queries to support your writing projects.

Introduction to using AI

Artificial Intelligence is quite the rage these days. It offers a lot of promise, but many of these promises are couched in technobabble and doublespeak and therefore are not understandable to people without specialized training. Youtube has many videos "explaining" AI, yet many of them remain incomprehensible to most viewers. What is often missing are practical applications that folks untrained in AI can use.

I've been writing since the last century. I've written short stories, novels and nonfiction books. I've self-published my books (except the first two) and I've marketed those books. In short, I know what writers and authors have to do.

My approach with this book is to provide writers and authors a practical guide to using

AI to support their work. AI is a complicated topic to master, and I've attempted to explain how to use it rather than write a technical manual on artificial intelligence.

The book contains examples of applications along with useful queries and the actual response from the AI program. Much of the content in this book is the actual AI responses to my queries.

All of the responses are provided by Perplexity.AI

The key to using an AI program is how you write the query. A generic query will produce a generic response. To get a more nuanced response, one must write a detailed and focused query. This isn't easy to do. Query Engineering is actually a field of study these days involving college level courses.

I have a number of queries and responses in this book on a number of topics. On first glance it may seem the queries and responses are redundant, but they are here for a reason: to provide practical examples of what AI can do. You can use the queries and responses as given. Simply copy them and use them for your own situation. For most writers and authors, I think I've covered the most common issues.

What this book covers

In October of 2023, I published a book called *Creating Your First Novel*. The premise of the book is that creating a book is a long-term, multi-phase project that will take years to complete. This graphic displays the five phases of the project.

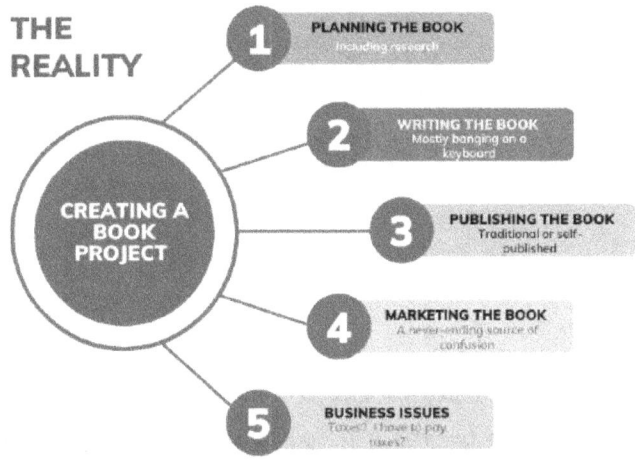

This fact is often a surprise to first-time authors.

While my book concentrated on a novel, this one changes the world "novel" to "book" since it addresses both fiction and nonfiction projects.

Another surprise to first-time authors is that planning and writing a book do little to prepare them for the publishing and marketing phases. The business issues often come as a further shock.

The intent of this book is to provide writers and authors with a framework that allows them to use Artificial Intelligence to support and assist their efforts in all five phases.

The reader may be surprised to learn that much of the text in this book is actual AI responses from Perplexity.AI, the program I used in developing this book. Those responses are shown in *italics* to separate it from my words.

So, what is AI anyway?

To get technical for a moment, below are two definitions I copied from the internet.

Artificial Intelligence (AI)

is a branch of computer science focused on creating machines that can perform tasks typically requiring human intelligence. This includes abilities like learning, reasoning, problem-solving, and understanding language.

How AI Works:

AI operates through algorithms that process large amounts of data. The technology often employs techniques like machine learning and deep learning, which allow computers to learn from experience and improve over time without explicit programming.

These definitions are not much use to the average writer and author. In this book, I'll mostly ignore the technical details and come up with practical applications writers and authors can use to support their work.

How AI programs work

AI programs appear to use magic to create responses. To get a basic understanding of how it processes queries, let's ask an AI program to describe what it does and how it processes a simple query.

If you aren't interested in understanding how AI programs work, you can safely skip to the next section.

Query:

Suppose I write a book summary and ask an AI program to generate a list of keywords for that book. Describe the process the AI program will go through to respond to the query.

Response:

When an AI program is asked to generate a list of keywords for a book based on its summary, it typically follows these steps:

1. Input Analysis

The AI receives the book summary as input, either through direct text entry or by analyzing uploaded files (e.g., PDFs, EPUBs) or URLs containing the summary.

It preprocesses the text by cleaning and tokenizing the content, breaking it into smaller units like words or phrases for analysis.

2. Keyword Extraction

Natural Language Processing (NLP): The AI uses NLP techniques to identify important words and phrases. This involves:

Frequency Analysis: Counting how often specific terms appear in the text to determine their relevance.

Part-of-Speech Tagging: Identifying nouns, verbs, and adjectives that are more likely to be keywords.

Contextual Relevance: Algorithms like TF-IDF (Term Frequency-Inverse Document Frequency) assess how unique a term is within the summary compared to general language usage.

Semantic Analysis: Advanced AI models (e.g., GPT-based systems) use contextual understanding to identify key themes, characters, and concepts that align with the book's genre or subject matter.

3. Keyword Optimization

If the output is intended for SEO purposes (e.g., for Amazon KDP), the AI integrates search-friendly terms based on user behavior and market trends. It ensures that keywords align with popular search queries related to the book's genre.

4. Output Generation

The AI compiles a list of keywords, often categorized by relevance or theme (e.g., plot elements, character names, settings).

Some tools allow customization of tone or focus, enabling users to refine the keyword list further.

5. Review and Export

The generated keywords can be reviewed interactively by the user for accuracy and relevance. Many platforms also allow exporting the list for use in marketing or metadata optimization.

This process ensures that the keywords are not only derived from the summary but also tailored to enhance discoverability and engagement.

I expect some readers will not understand this explanation, but we will experience keyword queries later in the book, so the explanation may become more germane later on.

Detailed Queries: the Key to Effectively Using AI

To use an AI program, you'll have to ask it specific questions or give it specific instructions on what it should do. These questions and instructions are known as "queries" or prompts.

In using AI, a general query will produce a bland response that isn't of much use. The response will be more or less what you get in any book on the topic. To get useful, unique responses, you must provide the AI program with detailed, unique queries. This requires a bit of practice.

To restate this, your query is how you communicate or 'talk' with an AI program. Remember, AI is just a piece of software and it will follow your instructions exactly. To get a useful reply from an AI program, your query must be precise.

Here is a quote from the book Generative AI for dummies. "To craft a successful prompt (or query), your request must be clear, provide enough context for the program to understand the direction and be creative enough to guide the program toward the desired outcome."

Here are a few examples of generic and detailed queries.

Example 1:

Generic query: What makes a character great?

Detailed query. What makes Ted Lasso a great character?

Example 2:

Generic query: I'm looking for a title for my new romance novel. Give me a list of possible titles

Detailed query: This is the synopsis of my new romance novel {insert synopsis} Give me a list of appropriate titles.

Example 3:

Generic query: I need plot ideas for my new

scifi novel. Give me some.

Detailed query. This is the storyline of my new scifi novel. {Insert storyline}. Generate appropriate plot events for this story.

Once the AI program responds to the query, it is the writer's job to determine what part of the response is useful for her project and what parts should be ignored or discarded.

Is AI safe to use and other concerns

One concern in today's environment is whether using an AI program is "safe." In other words, does the AI program use my data to build a profile or otherwise share my personal data and threads?

I use the Perplexity.AI program, and its response on data security is as follows: *Perplexity does not use your threads to build a personal profile unless you explicitly enable features like the "AI Data Usage" setting, which allows your data to improve the AI models. This feature can be turned off in the privacy settings, ensuring your data remains excluded from such processes. By default, your threads are private and only accessible to you.*

They are not shared on the internet unless you manually choose to make them public by sharing or converting them into a shareable page.

When asked about sharing threads online, Perplexity replied: *Perplexity AI may use your thread data to improve its AI models, but only if you have enabled the "AI Data Usage" setting in your account. This feature allows Perplexity to utilize your interactions to enhance search and model performance. However, you can opt out by turning off this setting in your profile, ensuring that your data is not used for AI improvement.*
Your threads are private by default and are not shared with others or made public unless you explicitly choose to share them via a sharable link. This ensures that your conversations remain confidential unless you decide otherwise.

In my opinion, using the Perplexity.AI program is safe.

Is this stuff ethical?

This book demonstrates a number of ways that writers and authors can use artificial intelligence in their daily routines with writing, publishing and marketing.

For writing applications, using AI to help develop characters and plots comes under the heading of providing models that can be used to augment the writer's thought processes. These models can save the writer a lot of time which can then be devoted to more creative work. These models can also trigger ideas that the writer can use

With publishing, the AI applications replace time-consuming 'donkey work.'

With marketing, AI provides solid marketing plans and ideas, but the author still must do the marketing work.

So, my answer to the question: **is this stuff ethical?** Yes, the queries and applications in this book are most certainly ethical. However, as a writer, you have a responsibility to disclose the extent of your AI usage.

Caveat
Caveat is a Latin word for "Beware!"

Artificial intelligence programs are not infallible. They are not magical nor always correct. Keep the following points in mind when using an AI app.

If you copy a query and reenter it into the same AI program, you will get a different response. The responses will be similar but different.

If you enter a query into two different AI apps (say, Perplexity and ChatGPT), you will get different responses. Upon inspection, the two responses will make similar points expressed differently, but each response will probably have points the other doesn't make.

If an AI app can't find an answer to your query, it will make up a response.

In other words, don't automatically assume the AI response is gospel. It ain't!

Using AI

Using an AI program to support your writing projects

A general question we all have (and the question that kicked off my lectures and this book) is "How can a writer utilize AI to support their writing projects?"

That's a great question. Let's take that question to an AI program and see what it says.

Query

How can a writer utilize AI to support their writing projects? Use an informal writing style.

Response:

Let's talk about something that might just blow your creative socks off: using AI to supercharge your writing. Now, before you roll your eyes and think, "Great, robots are coming for my job," hear me out. AI isn't here to replace your brilliant brain—it's here to be your sidekick, like Robin to your Batman or coffee to your late-night writing sessions.

Imagine you're stuck on a scene, and no amount of staring at the blinking cursor is helping. AI can toss out ideas, suggest dialogue, or even help you brainstorm plot twists you hadn't considered. Need to research something obscure without falling into an internet rabbit hole? AI's got your back. It can summarize info in seconds so you can stay focused on what really matters—your story.

It's also a lifesaver for those boring-but-necessary tasks, like editing, checking grammar, or rephrasing clunky sentences. Plus, it's great for experimenting with different tones or styles—want to make that blog post sound punchier? Done.

The best part? You're still the boss. AI is just a tool in your creative arsenal, helping you write faster, better, and with less stress. So why not give it a shot? Your future self (and deadlines) will thank you!

I couldn't have said it better! And yes, (surprise!) you can tell the AI program what writing style you want it to use. It can respond in an informal, sarcastic, stuffy, or literary style.

Let's go a bit deeper into the opening question. Below are three examples of how an

AI program can help writers:

- AI can be a powerful source of inspiration and help overcome creative blocks: AI tools can quickly generate ideas, concepts, and prompts to spark creativity.
- AI can assist in the initial stages of content creation: Writers can use AI to generate outlines, providing a starting point to refine and expand upon. AI can help with research by summarizing large amounts of information on a given topic.
- AI tools can enhance the editing process: Grammar and style checkers powered by AI can improve the technical aspects of writing. AI can help maintain consistency in tone, style, and voice throughout a piece.

This is not a comprehensive listing. There are other areas in which AI can help, but these are the most useful for writers and authors. AI programs excel at generating lists that can trigger creative sparks.

What should writers avoid doing when

using an AI program?

One neat trick that the AI programs are good at is providing negative information: Don'ts, in other words.

Let's try this query with an AI program and see what it says.

Query

What should writers avoid doing when using an AI program?

Response:

1. Relying on AI as a Replacement for Writing

Using AI to generate entire pieces of content without significant input or editing can undermine the writer's creative process and skill development. Writers risk becoming editors rather than creators, which stifles their unique voice and growth as writers.

2. Losing Authenticity and Personal Voice

AI-generated text often lacks the personal tone, style, and originality that make a writer's work distinctive. Readers value authentic perspectives and can feel "cheated" when they realize the content was AI-generated.

3. Overlooking Ethical Transparency

Passing off AI-generated work as entirely original without disclosure can be seen as deceptive. Ethical concerns arise when writers fail to inform readers about the extent of AI's involvement in their work.

4. Accepting AI Output Without Critical Review

AI can produce generic, repetitive, or inaccurate content. Writers must carefully edit and fact-check AI-generated material to ensure quality and factual accuracy, especially in specialized or sensitive topics like health or finance.

5. Allowing AI to Replace Creativity

Relying too heavily on AI for idea generation or storytelling risks producing formulaic or derivative work. True creativity involves exploring unique perspectives and emotions—qualities that AI cannot replicate].

6. Failing to Use AI as a Tool for Enhancement

Writers should use AI to enhance their craft (e.g., brainstorming, editing, or improving clarity) rather than as a shortcut to replace effort. Properly leveraging AI requires thoughtful prompts and substantial human input.

Phase 1: Planning

The planning phase of writing is a critical stage where ideas are conceived, organized, and refined. In this initial phase, the assistance of artificial intelligence can prove invaluable. AI programs offer a suite of tools designed to enhance creativity and streamline the planning process, making them indispensable companions for writers and authors.

Whether you seek to organize your thoughts, brainstorm fresh ideas, develop compelling characters, or construct intricate plots, AI can assist in each of these areas. AI can generate suggestions that might not have been considered otherwise, providing a new perspective that can enrich your creative process

In this section, I will demonstrate how AI tools can help structure your narrative, inspire innovative concepts, and aid in the meticulous crafting of characters and storylines.

By integrating AI into your writing practice,

you can enhance your productivity and creativity, ultimately leading to more polished and engaging works of literature.

Research

An AI tool is an ideal resource to aid in researching a book or topic within a book. Here's what an AIi prompt and the response look like:

Query:

How can writers and authors use AI for research?

Response:

Writers and authors can leverage AI tools to enhance their research and writing processes in several impactful ways:

1. Research Support

Finding Sources: AI-powered tools like Semantic Scholar, Elicit, and Perplexity can help locate academic papers, articles, or other resources efficiently, reducing the time spent on manual searches.

Summarizing Information: AI tools like ChatGPT or Elicit can summarize research papers, websites, or historical contexts, aiding in quickly assessing the relevance of a source.

Analyzing Content: Advanced AI tools can interrogate research papers or websites by answering specific questions about their content or identifying patterns across multiple sources.

Citation Management: Tools like Zotero and EndNote assist in organizing references and generating citations in various styles.

2. Idea Generation and Structuring

Overcoming Writer's Block: AI can suggest creative ideas, themes, character arcs, or even plot structures based on a writer's input, helping to kickstart projects.

Outlining: AI tools like ChatGPT can create detailed outlines for books, articles, or research papers, providing a roadmap for the writing process.

Concept Mapping: Tools such as Research Rabbit and Aria (a Zotero plugin) help visualize connections between ideas or research topics.

3. Drafting and Editing

Draft Creation: Writers can use AI to generate drafts for specific sections of their work, such as introductions or summaries. These drafts serve as starting points for refinement.

Language Enhancement: AI-powered writing assistants offer real-time grammar corrections, stylistic improvements, and tone adjustments to enhance readability and professionalism.

Feedback on Arguments: AI can review drafts to identify logical inconsistencies or gaps in arguments.

4. Data Analysis and Visualization

AI tools can analyze datasets and create narratives or visualizations from them, making it easier to incorporate data-driven insights into written work.

5. Ethical Considerations

Writers must disclose the use of AI tools transparently in their work to maintain ethical standards. They are fully responsible for verifying the accuracy and originality of AI-generated content.

By integrating these capabilities into their workflow while maintaining creativity and authenticity, writers can significantly enhance productivity and innovation without compromising the human essence of storytelling or analysis.

That is rather long way to say that, yes, AI can be a useful tool when it comes to researching a project.

Brainstorming

Brainstorming is one of the great applications of an AI program. You can use it when you're stuck for ideas, when trying to flesh out a concept and for many more applications. To demonstrate the brainstorming feature, let's use AI.

Query

How can AI be used to brainstorm?

Response

AI can significantly enhance the brainstorming process by providing new perspectives, speeding up idea generation, and improving creativity. Here's how AI can be used effectively in brainstorming sessions:

1. Data Input and Processing

Input Prompts: Users start by inputting a prompt, question, or context into the AI system. This serves as the foundation for generating ideas.

AI Processing: The AI uses machine learning algorithms and natural language processing to analyze patterns and relationships within its data.

2. Idea Generation

Creative Suggestions: Based on its analysis, AI generates creative suggestions, ideas, or solutions related to the input prompt. This output can range from text-based responses to more complex suggestions.

Exploring Scenarios: AI can explore "what-if" scenarios and provide various plot directions or solutions that users can refine and develop further.

3. Collaboration and Iteration

Human Collaboration: The generated ideas are presented to users who evaluate, refine, and build upon them. Human judgment is crucial for selecting the best ideas.

Feedback Loop: Engaging in a feedback loop with AI allows users to continuously refine their ideas based on AI's suggestions.

4. Enhancing Creativity

Overcoming Writer's Block: AI can offer continuous prompts and ideas to help overcome creative barriers like writer's block.

Diverse Perspectives: By analyzing large datasets, AI can offer various perspectives that humans might not consider, thus enhancing creativity.

5. Efficiency and Productivity

Rapid Idea Generation: AI can quickly generate a large number of ideas, saving time and allowing teams to focus on refining the most promising one.

Structured Brainstorming: AI-driven tools can facilitate a more structured brainstorming process by providing real-time analysis of discussions.

6. Applications in Various Fields

Storytelling and Writing: Writers can use AI to brainstorm story ideas, develop characters, and structure plots by generating prompts based on themes or genres.

Business Strategy: Business leaders can use AI to explore multiple approaches for strategic decisions or problem-solving.

In conclusion, while AI can greatly enhance the brainstorming process by providing speed, diversity, and structure, it is most effective when used in collaboration with human creativity and judgment.

Here's more about brainstorming.

Query

Create a list of typical brainstorming ideas writers and authors can use.

Response

Here is a list of typical brainstorming techniques that writers and authors can use to generate creative ideas:

Brainstorming Techniques

1. Word Vomit (Freewriting)

Let words flow without inhibition to overcome self-doubt and unlock creativity.

2. Bullet Points

Create structured lists to outline plot, characters, and settings, focusing on key elements without worrying about details.

3. The Plot Grid

Organize plot points visually to see the story's structure and identify gaps or opportunities for development.

4. Connecting Branches

Link different story elements like scenes, characters, and settings to create a cohesive narrative.

5. Mind Mapping

Use diagrams to organize thoughts and explore connections between ideas, facilitating a "brain dump" of concepts.

6. Starbursting

Explore a topic by asking questions like Who? What? Where? When? Why? How? helping to uncover different angles.

7. Lists or Bullets

Jot down ideas as they come in simple words or phrases, then review and expand upon them.

8. What If? Questions

Pose hypothetical scenarios to explore different story outcomes and develop plot ideas.

9. Genre Exploration

Consider the genres you enjoy writing or reading and brainstorm how to reimagine their elements creatively

10. Loglines

Develop a one- or two-sentence pitch for your story idea to flesh out its basic elements and test its potential.

These techniques can help writers overcome creative blocks and generate new ideas for their stories.

What questions do you want to ask AI on brainstorming? Perhaps you have an idea that's begging to be explored. Write an AI query and explore it. Use the queries above and modify them to suit your needs or use this one:

Query

I have an idea about {enter idea description}. Expand the idea by brainstorming possible {applications/ expansions/variations}.

Creating a nonfiction outline

A large part of writing a nonfiction book is coming up with an outline. Can AI help? Let's find out.

Query:

I plan to write a nonfiction book called Creating Your First Novel that will describe the five phases involved in creating a novel: planning, writing, publishing, marketing and author business. Generate an outline for the book. The book is nonfiction and doesn't require characters or a plot.

Response:

(Author note: The response is lengthy and broken down by the phases listed in the query)

Introduction

Planning the book

Chapters 1-3

Writing

Chapters 4-6

Publishing

Chapters 7-9

Marketing

Chapters 10-12

Author business

Chapters 13-14
Conclusion
Appendices

Each chapter came with an explanation of what could go into that chapter.

This query gave me some trouble. The query above is the third one I tried. With the first two, AI thought I was writing a novel and gave me a response with character and plot development. The last line in the query finally got AI straightened out. Lesson learned: how you structure the query is very important. If you mislead the AI program, the response will be rubbish. This demonstrates that writers should not accept a response without verifying it. And be careful how you phrase the queries.

Plotting

Now I'll turn to plots and what AI can do for the writer who has a brief story concept and is looking for plot ideas.

Query

I want to write a story that involves Shakespeare's plays Hamlet and Othello turned into comedies, with Falstaff as a con artist who sees both protagonists as easy marks. Can you develop a plot for this story?

Response

Plot Outline for a Comedic Story Featuring Falstaff, Hamlet, and Othello

Title: Falstaff's Follies: A Comedy of Errors in Elsinore and Venice

Setting

The story is set in a whimsical, alternate Shakespearean universe where the tragedies of Hamlet and Othello are reimagined as comedies. The action takes place in both Elsinore Castle and the bustling streets of Venice.

Main Characters

• Falstaff: A roguish con artist with a penchant for elaborate schemes.

• Hamlet: The melancholic prince of Denmark, easily distracted by philosophical musings.

• Othello: A noble but gullible general in Venice.

• Iago: Othello's cunning but now bumbling ensign.

• Polonius: The verbose and comically oblivious advisor to King Claudius.

• Desdemona: Othello's spirited wife, who is wise to Falstaff's antics.

Plot Summary
Act 1: The Scheme Begins

Falstaff arrives in Elsinore, having heard of Hamlet's indecisiveness and sees an opportunity to exploit the prince's existential crises for profit. He poses as a wise philosopher who can help Hamlet find the meaning of life. Meanwhile, in Venice, Falstaff learns of Othello's jealousy issues and decides to sell him a "magic" potion that supposedly reveals the truth about one's spouse.

Act 2: Chaos in Elsinore

In Elsinore, Falstaff's antics lead to a series of misunderstandings. Polonius becomes convinced that Falstaff is a spy, while Hamlet starts questioning everything around him even more fervently. Falstaff orchestrates a fake haunting in the castle to convince Hamlet that his father's ghost demands he buy more "philosophical consultations."

Act 3: Venetian Misadventures

Falstaff travels to Venice, where he encounters Iago. Mistaking Iago for an ally, Falstaff sells him the "magic" potion intended for Othello. Iago, ever eager to manipulate others, uses it on Othello, leading to a series of comedic errors where Othello becomes suspicious of everyone except Desdemona.

Act 4: The Great Unraveling

Back in Elsinore, Falstaff's schemes begin to unravel as Hamlet accidentally uncovers the truth about the fake haunting. In Venice, Desdemona cleverly exposes Falstaff's con by staging her own comedic play within a play, revealing Iago's foolishness.

Act 5: Resolution and Revelry

Realizing he has been outwitted by both Desdemona and Hamlet, Falstaff decides to come clean. He admits his tricks but charms everyone with his wit and humor. In the spirit of reconciliation, Hamlet invites everyone to Elsinore for a grand feast. The story ends with laughter and merriment as all characters join together in celebration.

Themes

The Absurdity of Human Nature: Highlighting how easily people can be fooled by their desires and fears.

Redemption through Humor: Demonstrating how laughter can resolve conflicts and bring people together.

The Power of Wit and Wisdom: Showcasing how cleverness can outmaneuver deceit.

This comedic retelling blends elements from both Hamlet and Othello, transforming their *tragic elements into sources of humor while maintaining the charm of Shakespearean storytelling.*

The response is voluminous, but it provides some cool ideas. The plot for my novel *Falstaff's Big Gamble* is quite different from these ideas, but some of them are on the mark. If I were starting from scratch, the novel would have likely had a few of these ideas incorporated into it.

What AI provides in this case is a starting point to develop your plot and story. It's the writer's job to choose the items that fit into their concept of a story and ignore the rest.

Here is an interesting observation about using an Ai app. In my query, I didn't specify the location of the story or the setting. In this case, Ai made one up: Elsinore. Ai apps are known to invent responses when the query doesn't give them enough information. This clearly demonstrates a danger in accepting an AI response without being skeptical about it.

An AI program can also be used to analyze an existing story. This is a useful exercise to learn more about developing plots.

Optional plot query

Analyze the plot of {enter story title}.

Character traits

Let's begin with a general query about character development and see what AI has to say about it.

Query

What traits should a writer cultivate to create compelling and multidimensional characters?

Response

To create compelling and well-rounded characters, a writer should focus on developing several key traits and aspects. Here are some important traits and considerations to keep in mind:

Key Traits for Character Development

1. Worldview and Beliefs

Characters should have a distinct worldview shaped by their religious, philosophical, and political beliefs. This affects how they perceive the world and interact with others.

2. Physical Traits

Consider the character's physical appearance, as it can influence how other characters perceive them and how they fit into the story's setting.

3. Morals and Values

Define what morals guide your characters and what they value most. These can drive their decisions and actions throughout the story.

4. Goals and Motivations

Characters need compelling goals and motivations that drive the plot forward. Understanding what a character wants is crucial for developing their arc.

5. Strengths and Weaknesses

Every character should have both strengths and weaknesses. These traits add depth and make characters relatable, as they reflect real human complexity.

6. Social Traits

Consider how your character interacts socially. Are they extroverted or introverted? Their social behavior can add depth to their personality.

7. Emotional Depth

Characters should have emotional traits that influence their reactions to events in the story. This includes understanding their fears, hopes, and desires.

8. Backstory

A character's past shapes their present behavior and decisions. Knowing their history helps in crafting realistic responses to situations.

Tips for Developing Characters

Holistic Approach: Think of characters as whole beings rather than a list of traits. This helps in creating more believable characters.

- *Character Arc: Ensure your characters undergo a transformation or growth throughout the story, which makes their journey engaging.*
- *Conflict Creation: Use traits to create conflict or synergy among characters, which can drive the narrative forward.*
- *Show, Don't Tell: Instead of listing traits, show them through actions, dialogue, and decisions within the story context.*
- *Reader Connection: Develop traits that allow readers to empathize or connect with characters on an emotional level.*

By focusing on these elements, writers can create rich, multidimensional characters that resonate with readers and enhance the storytelling experience.

This is quite a list, but it is a general list that can be found in most books on fiction writing. Still, in a book, the information would be spread out over many pages or even chapters. It's useful to have a summary like this for reference and to keep handy.

Ted Lasso

This is where AI queries can really shine. Suppose you want your main character to be like Ted Lasso. In this case you want to know what makes Ted a great character. So you write a query.

Ted Lasso is just an example. You can use any character from TV, movies or literature. Or maybe even history if you want your character to be like, say, Napoleon or Boudicca

AI Query:

What makes Ted Lasso a great character?

AI Response:

Ted Lasso is a compelling character for several reasons, rooted in his unique approach to leadership, his authentic personality, and his ability to inspire those around him.

Core Traits

Authenticity and Kindness: Ted embodies genuine kindness and warmth. He treats everyone with respect and empathy, regardless of how he is treated in return. His authenticity shines through in his interactions, making people feel valued and understood.

Optimism and Joy: Ted's infectious optimism and joy set him apart. He maintains a positive outlook even in challenging situations, which inspires hope and resilience in those around him. This positivity is not superficial; it is deeply rooted in his belief in the potential of others.

Emotional Intelligence: Ted's emotional health is a standout trait. He is empathetic, curious rather than judgmental, and understands the importance of forgiving and moving on quickly—symbolized by his 'be a goldfish philosophy'.

Leadership Style

Inclusive Leadership: Ted focuses on building strong relationships within his team. He invests time in understanding each individual, fostering a sense of belonging and mutual respect. His leadership style emphasizes teamwork, inclusion, and personal growth over mere performance metrics.

Empowerment through Humor: Ted uses humor to diffuse tension and build camaraderie. His witty remarks and light-hearted approach make him approachable and relatable, helping to break down barriers between him and others.

Impact on Others

Transformative Influence: Ted's presence has a transformative effect on those around him. His belief in people encourages them to become better versions of themselves. He creates an environment where individuals feel safe to express themselves and take risks without fear of judgment.

Forgiveness and Understanding: Ted practices quick forgiveness, understanding that holding onto grudges hinders progress. His ability to forgive even when wronged demonstrates his deep understanding of human nature and the importance of moving forward.

In summary, Ted Lasso's greatness as a character lies in his unwavering belief in people, his joyful approach to life, and his ability to lead with empathy and authenticity. These qualities not only make him an effective coach but also an inspiring figure who resonates with audiences worldwide. This response provides the writer with a model to use in her own character development

I think this response speaks for itself and I have nothing to add to it.

Jackson Lamb

Let's try to get another character model, this time using Jackson Lamb, the complicated main character from the TV series *Slow Horses*.

Query

I want to model my character after Jackson Lamb. How do I do that?

Response

Jackson Lamb, the protagonist of Mick Herron's *Slough House* series, is celebrated as one of the most compelling characters in modern spy fiction due to his unique blend of contradictions, sharp intellect, and dark humor.

Key Traits That Make Jackson Lamb a Great Character:

1. Unlikely Hero: Lamb defies the archetype of a polished spy hero. He is slovenly, abrasive, and crude, with poor hygiene and a penchant for offensive remarks. Yet beneath this off-putting exterior lies a brilliant mind and an unparalleled understanding of espionage, honed during his Cold War days as an elite MI5 operative.

2. Complex Morality: Lamb operates in

morally gray territory. While he often belittles and mocks his team of "Slow Horses" (disgraced MI5 agents relegated to Slough House), he fiercely protects them when they are threatened. His cynicism toward bureaucracy and political corruption adds depth to his character, making him both a rebel and a deeply loyal leader.

3. Strategic Genius: Lamb's slovenly demeanor is a deliberate facade that allows him to work unnoticed and underestimated. He is always several steps ahead of both allies and adversaries, using his sharp wit and deep experience to outmaneuver bureaucratic rivals like Diana Taverner and external threats alike.

4. Dark Humor and Sarcasm: Lamb's biting humor and relentless sarcasm provide levity in the otherwise grim world of espionage. His "combat sarcasm" often masks his deeper care for his team while keeping others off balance.

5. Emotional Complexity: Despite his gruffness, Lamb shows glimpses of humanity. His past traumas, such as being forced to kill his mentor for betrayal, have shaped his jaded outlook on life and work. This emotional depth makes him relatable despite his many flaws.

6. Charismatic Portrayal: Gary Oldman's portrayal of Jackson Lamb in Apple TV+'s

Slow Horses has further elevated the character. Oldman captures Lamb's contradictions—his laziness masking brilliance and cruelty hiding reluctant compassion—making him one of the most memorable characters on television today.

In sum, Jackson Lamb is a masterfully crafted antihero whose sharp intellect, moral ambiguity, and sardonic wit make him unforgettable in both literature and television. His flaws are not just tolerated but celebrated as essential elements of his brilliance and humanity.

Once again, you have a model to use in your own character development.

Other characters

Here is an optional activity. Once you get an AI program working and understand how to write queries, use it to explore what makes these characters great.

Yossarian (from Catch-22)

Cynical and paranoid bomber pilot in World War II

Driven by a strong desire to stay alive in the face of absurd military bureaucracy

Struggles with the paradoxical "Catch-22" that keeps him trapped in combat duty

Richard Sharpe (from Bernard Cornwell's novels)

Historical fiction hero set during the Napoleonic Wars

Rises from private to lieutenant colonel through a series of adventures

Brave and resourceful character who appeals to readers of military

fiction

Frodo Baggins (from Lord of the Rings)

Unlikely hero chosen to bear the burden of the One Ring

Possesses inner strength and purity of heart that sets him apart from others

Struggles with the temptation of the Ring's power throughout his journey

Inspector Clouseau (from the Pink Panther movies)

Bumbling yet confident French detective

Known for his comical mishaps and exaggerated French accent

Solves cases through luck rather than skill, often to the frustration of his superiors

You can add your own favorite characters. Print and save these responses because they will form your own master class on how to develop a great character.

Phase 2: Writing

There isn't much AI can do for a writer in this phase, but AI can assist with the editing and rewriting process.

In this phase, you spend much of your time banging on a keyword or staring out the window or cursing at the screen. If this is your first book, your family might think you're playing computer games (until you produce a manuscript).

Let's see what AI suggests about what not to do.

What should fiction writers avoid doing while writing the first draft?

Query

What should fiction writers avoid doing while writing the first draft?

Response

When writing the first draft of a novel, fiction writers should avoid several common pitfalls to enhance their creative process and ensure a more effective drafting phase. Here are key points to consider:

Avoid Perfectionism

Resist the Urge to Edit: One of the most significant mistakes is editing while writing. This can hinder the natural flow of ideas and lead to frustration and writer's block. The first draft is meant to be rough and unpolished, serving as a foundation for future revisions.

Embrace the Messiness

Accept Imperfections: The first draft is often messy, with bad grammar, disjointed ideas, and incomplete thoughts. Writers should allow themselves to produce this "ugly duckling" without fear of judgment. This approach helps in capturing the essence of the story, which can be refined later.

Focus on Completion

Prioritize Finishing Over Quality: The primary goal of a first draft is to complete it. Writers should not worry about style, word choice, or even plot holes at this stage. Completing the draft provides a comprehensive view of the story, making subsequent revisions more focused and effective.

Avoid Over-planning

Balance Planning and Discovery: While some planning is necessary, writers should not get bogged down in trying to perfect every scene or character detail before writing. Allowing room for discovery can lead to unexpected and exciting developments in the story.

Manage Expectations

Don't Aim for a Final Product: Writers should not expect their first draft to be publish-ready. Understanding that multiple drafts are part of the process helps in managing expectations and reducing anxiety about imperfections.

By avoiding these pitfalls, fiction writers can focus on capturing their creative ideas without the pressure of perfection, ultimately leading to a more rewarding writing process.

Here is a general query for you nonfiction writers

Query

What should nonfiction writers avoid doing

while writing the first draft?

Response

When writing the first draft of a nonfiction book, writers should avoid several common pitfalls to ensure a more productive and creative process:

Avoid Perfectionism

1. Resist the Urge to Edit: One of the biggest mistakes is trying to perfect grammar, spelling, and punctuation during the first draft. This can hinder creativity and flow, leading to a superficial and uninspired manuscript. Editing should be reserved for later drafts.

2. Embrace Imperfection: Accept that the first draft will be rough and messy. This phase is about getting ideas down on paper, not creating a polished piece. Allow yourself to write poorly; this freedom can lead to discovering your true voice.

Avoid Overplanning

1. Don't Write in Sequential Order: It's not necessary to start with the introduction or follow a strict order. Jumping around can help maintain momentum and allow for spontaneous creativity.

2. Avoid Getting Stuck on Details: Focus on the broader structure rather than getting bogged down in details like chapter length or perfect descriptions. These can be refined in later drafts.

Avoid Self-Criticism

1. Silence the Inner Critic: Writers often sabotage themselves by being overly critical of their work, which can lead to writer's block. It's important to push through self-doubt and keep writing.

2. Don't Compare Yourself to Others: Comparing your work to successful authors can be discouraging. Remember that all published books have undergone extensive revisions.

By avoiding these common pitfalls, nonfiction writers can create a more effective and enjoyable first draft process, laying a strong foundation for future revisions.

Titles

Ai programs can suggest appropriate titles for a book provided you give the program sufficient information in your query.

Query

My fantasy story is a Shakespearean spoof combining the Hamlet and Othello plays and turning them into comedies with Falstaff as the

bad guy. Create a list of possible titles for the
story.

Actual response:

- *Falstaff's Follies: A Comedy of Errors,*
- *Falstaff's Misadventures,*
- *The Pranks of Prince Hamlet and Othello,*
- *Laughing with the Moor and the Dane,*
- *The Bard's Buffoonery: Falstaff's
  Revenge*

By now, you are getting the idea about queries
and gaining a sense of how to structure them

Editing

AI apps can edit a piece of your writing. In
this case the appropriate query can be quite
simple.

Query

Edit the following piece: {paste text here}

Or you can give AI more specific
instructions.

Query

Edit the following piece and point out
examples where show-don't-tell can be used
{paste text here}.

Response

(I fed the AI a piece of writing from an inexperienced writer I know and this is part of the response.)

Suggestions for "Show-Don't-Tell" Improvements

- *Helene's resentment toward laundry:*
Instead of saying "she hated that task" or "she thought herself above it," show Helene's disdain through actions or internal dialogue:
Example: Helene wrinkled her nose as she pulled another damp shirt from the basket. "I should be sipping tea while someone else does this," she muttered under her breath.

- *Helene's financial frustrations:*
Rather than explicitly stating "Her monetary means showed otherwise," you could show how tight finances affected their lives:
Example: The worn-out washing machine clanked noisily in protest as it spun the last load—a reminder that replacing it would have to wait until next year.

- *Helene's nosiness:*
Instead of saying "From childhood on, she was always nosy," show this trait through behavior:
Example: Her fingers hovered over the drawer handle for only a moment before curiosity won out—it always did.

• Anita's reaction to finding the gray hair:
Instead of saying "she felt disappointment and disgust," show these emotions through physical reactions or internal thoughts:

Example: Anita's jaw tightened as she stared at the strand of gray hair glinting against the dark fabric of her jeans. Her hands curled into fists at her sides as heat rose in her cheeks.

• Anita's longing for privacy:
Rather than stating "Can't anything belong solely to herself?" show this through symbolic actions or imagery:

Example: She slammed the drawer shut with more force than intended, wishing for walls thicker than paper and locks stronger than trust.

By using more sensory details and character actions instead of directly stating feelings or traits, you can create a richer and more immersive narrative!

I had a problem with editing queries: I couldn't see what the AI changed unless I examined both word for word. A solution to this issue is to add the following statement to your editing queries: Highlight your changes.

Rewriting

AI apps can be used to rewrite scenes, articles, letters and whatever. Here is an example. I took a paragraph from an article I wrote, pasted it into Perplexity.AI and gave the app a set of instructions.

Query

Rewrite this paragraph two different ways: one in a light-hearted tone, one in a pompous tone: Self-publishing a book is a complex project. It gets even more complex when you add in the necessary pre-publication marketing tasks. The best way to proceed with a project like this is by using a detailed plan. This article describes such a plan in brief.

Response

Light-Hearted Tone

Publishing your own book is no walk in the park—it's more like a hike up a mountain with a backpack full of snacks and surprises. And just when you think you've reached the summit, here comes pre-publication marketing to add a little extra weight! But don't worry, the best way to tackle this adventure is with a trusty map (a.k.a. a detailed plan). Lucky for you, this article gives you the lowdown on how to get started!

Pompous Tone

Ah, the noble endeavor of self-publishing—a veritable odyssey of intellectual labor and creative ambition. Yet, as if crafting the manuscript were not Herculean enough, one must also contend with the labyrinthine intricacies of pre-publication marketing. Fear not, for the sagacious path forward lies in the meticulous construction of a master plan. This article, in its wisdom, deigns to outline such a plan for your enlightenment.

This offers intriguing possibilities, doesn't it?

Let's say you're writing a scene and you find your main character stuck in a traffic jam. This is a critical part of the story and the guy has to get to a point a mile away in only a few minutes or else bad things will happen.

Query. My character is in traffic jam and it's urgent that he rescue someone in a few minutes. Tell me five ways he can get out or around the traffic jam.

Response

If your character is in a traffic jam and urgently needs to rescue someone in just a few minutes, here are five practical ways they can navigate or bypass the traffic jam:

1. Use Navigation Apps for Alternate Routes

Leverage navigation apps like Waze or Google Maps to identify alternative routes. These apps provide real-time updates and can suggest less congested back roads or detours to avoid the traffic jam.

2. Switch to a Motorcycle, Bicycle, or On Foot

If the character has access to a motorcycle or bicycle, they can maneuver through traffic more easily. Alternatively, if the destination is close enough, abandoning the vehicle and proceeding on foot might be quicker.

3. Utilize Emergency Vehicle Privileges (if Applicable)

If the character is a first responder or has access to an emergency vehicle, they could use sirens and lights to navigate through traffic legally and safely. This approach requires adherence to local traffic laws.

4. Take Advantage of Sidewalks or Shoulders (Cautiously)

In extreme situations, driving on the shoulder of the road or even using sidewalks (if safe and legal) could help bypass the jam. However, this should only be done if it does not endanger pedestrians or violate strict laws.

5. Call for Assistance

If none of the above options work, contacting local authorities for assistance might help. Police or emergency services could clear a path if the rescue is critical and time-sensitive.

These strategies depend on the urgency of the situation, available resources, and local regulations. The character must balance urgency with safety and legality in their decision-making.

But what if your story is a comedy? The above options are rather bland and un-humorous. So let's change the query to request humorous solutions.

Query

My character is in traffic jam, and it's urgent that he rescue someone in a few minutes. Tell me five humorous ways he can get out or around the traffic jam.

Response

Here are five humorous and creative ways your character could escape a traffic jam in their urgent quest to rescue someone:

1. Helium Balloon Lift-Off

*Your character stumbles upon a vendor selling giant helium balloons. They tie enough balloons to their car to "float" it above the traffic (à la *Up*). While it's obviously impractical, the sight of a car hovering over the jam is sure to cause confusion and laughter among fellow drivers.*

2. The Sidewalk Sprinter

Frustrated with the gridlock, your character abandons their car, grabs a pair of rollerblades or a scooter from the trunk, and zips down the sidewalk like a determined delivery driver. Bonus points if they yell, "Coming through! Hero on a mission!"

3. Traffic Jam DJ Takeover

Your character hacks into the local radio station and broadcasts an emergency message: "Attention drivers! Free donuts ahead if you clear this lane!" The ensuing chaos creates just enough space for them to maneuver through.

4. Carpool Karaoke Escape Plan

*They convince everyone stuck in traffic to start singing a ridiculously catchy song together (like *Baby Shark*). The collective distraction causes drivers to inch forward unconsciously, clearing the jam just enough for your character to weave through.*

5. Invisible Cloak of Authority

Your character dons an orange vest and grabs a random traffic cone from their trunk. Pretending to be an official, they redirect cars into nonsensical patterns until they've cleared their own path forward. The other drivers are too confused to argue!

These humorous scenarios not only add levity but also showcase your character's resourcefulness and determination in a pinch!

Together these two queries and responses illustrate another useful application of AI.

Phase 3: Publishing

While AI can play a role in seeking out agents and publishers, it has a far bigger role in the self-publishing process. This is especially true when it comes to the tedious work involved in a self-publishing project such as coming up with keywords, categories and more. The AI program can save. an author a lot of non-creative time, which means in turn more time for creative activities.

Fiction query letters

Query letters are an integral part of seeking publication via an agent of a publisher. A great query letter is the best way to approach these organizations. Let's see what an AI query can produce.

General Query

My {title} is a {genre} book about {brief

description}. Write a query letter targeted at an agent.

Actual query

My Falstaff's Big Gamble is a humorous fantasy retelling of Shakespeare's Hamlet and Othello plays. Write a query letter targeted at an agent.

{Note: I used one of my published books in this example and AI found references to it online}

Fiction response

[Your Name]
[Your Address]
[City, State, Zip Code]
[Email Address]
[Phone Number]
[Date]

[Agent's Name]
[Agency's Name]
[Agency's Address]
[City, State, Zip Code]

Dear [Agent's Name],

I am seeking representation for my humorous fantasy novel, "Falstaff's Big

Gamble," a unique retelling of Shakespeare's "Hamlet" and "Othello" with a comedic twist. This manuscript, complete at [word count], combines the wit of classic Shakespearean characters with the charm of a fantastical world filled with trolls, dwarfs, and elves.

Falstaff's Big Gamble takes readers on an adventurous journey where familiar tragedies are transformed into comedies. The story follows Falstaff on a high-seas hunt for pirates while his sidekick, Poulet, embarks on a romantic subplot. The novel cleverly intertwines elements from "Hamlet," "Othello," and even "Macbeth," creating a quirky and engaging narrative that pays homage to Shakespeare while offering something fresh and entertaining for modern readers.

The book has been well-received by reviewers. Kirkus Reviews noted its humorous approach to classic characters, while Readers Favorite praised its appeal to both Shakespeare enthusiasts and newcomers alike. This novel is perfect for readers who enjoy fantasy adventures with a comedic edge, akin to works by authors like Craig Shaw Gardner and John Morressy.

I am an author with over forty published short stories and several nonfiction articles. My passion lies in crafting stories that blend humor with speculative fiction, as seen in my previous works such as Wotan's Dilemma.

I have included [materials you are including: synopsis, sample chapters, etc.] per your submission guidelines. Thank you for considering my query. I look forward to the possibility of working together.

Warm regards,

[Your Name]

It is now your responsibility to edit and revise this query letter to be more relevant to your situation.

Nonfiction query letters
General Query
My {title} is a nonfiction book about {brief description}. Write a query letter targeted at an agent.

Actual query

My Creating Your First Novel is a nonfiction book that describes and explains the five phases of creating a book: planning, writing, publishing, marketing and author business. Write a query letter targeted at an agent.

Response

[Your Name]
[Your Address]
[City, State, ZIP Code]
[Your Email Address]
[Your Phone Number]
[Date]

[Agent's Name]
[Agency's Name]
[Agency's Address]
[City, State, ZIP Code]

Dear [Agent's Name],

I am seeking representation for my nonfiction book, *Creating Your First Novel*, a comprehensive guide that demystifies the journey from idea to publication for aspiring novelists. With the growing interest in self-publishing and the increasing number of writers looking to break into the market, this *book provides essential insights into the five critical phases of creating a successful novel: planning, writing, publishing, marketing, and managing the author business.*

Creating Your First Novel is designed to empower new writers with practical advice and actionable strategies. The book begins with the Planning phase, offering tools to help writers develop compelling story ideas and outlines. In the Writing phase, I delve into techniques for maintaining motivation and crafting engaging prose. The Publishing section guides readers through traditional and self-publishing options, helping them choose the best path for their work. The Marketing phase provides innovative strategies for building an audience and promoting a book effectively. Finally, the Author Business chapter equips writers with knowledge about managing their careers as professional authors.

With over [X years] of experience in the publishing industry and having worked with numerous bestselling authors, I bring a wealth of knowledge to this project. My background includes [briefly mention any relevant experience or credentials], which has given me unique insights into what makes a book successful in today's competitive market.

I believe Creating Your First Novel will appeal to both novice writers and those who have attempted writing before but need guidance to navigate the complexities of the publishing world. Comparable titles include On Writing by Stephen King and Bird by Bird by Anne Lamott, yet my book stands out by offering a holistic approach that addresses not only the craft of writing but also the business aspects of being an author.

I am submitting this proposal to you because of your interest in nonfiction works that inspire and educate readers. I admire your work with [mention any specific authors or books the agent has represented that are relevant], and I believe my book aligns well with your expertise.

Thank you for considering my proposal. I have included [mention any enclosed materials like a proposal or sample chapters if applicable]. I look forward to the possibility of working together to bring *Creating Your First Novel* to aspiring authors everywhere.

Warm regards,

[Your Name]
Make sure to personalize this template with specific details about your experience, any comparable books, and why you chose this particular agent. Good luck!

It is now your responsibility to edit and revise this query letter to make it more relevant to your situation.

What do self-publishing authors often do wrong

Before we begin to explore how AI can be used for self-publishing a book, let's find out what self-publishing authors do wrong (sometimes).

Query

What do self-publishing authors often do wrong?

Response

Self-publishing authors often encounter several common pitfalls that can hinder the success of their books. Here are some of the most frequent mistakes and how to avoid them

1. Inadequate Research and Planning

Mistake: Many authors fail to thoroughly research the self-publishing process, which can affect budgeting, marketing, and the overall quality of the book.

Solution: Authors should develop a comprehensive understanding of the self-publishing process, including market research, to better plan their publishing journey.

2. Skipping Professional Editing

Mistake: To save money or due to overconfidence in their writing, some authors skip professional editing, leading to errors that can damage their credibility.

Solution: Investing in professional editing services is crucial. If budget constraints exist, consider hiring freelance editors or trading services with other writers.

3. Poor Cover Design

Mistake: Some authors neglect the importance of a professionally designed book cover, which can deter potential readers.

Solution: Hire a professional cover designer who understands genre conventions and can create an appealing cover that attracts your target audience.

4. Ineffective Marketing Strategy

Mistake: Authors often assume that readers will find their book organically without a solid marketing plan].

Solution: Develop a comprehensive marketing strategy before launching the book. This includes building an author platform, engaging with readers through social media, and utilizing paid advertising options.

5. Rushing the Editing Process

Mistake: In a hurry to publish, authors may rush through the editing process, resulting in a poorly edited manuscript.

Solution: Take the necessary time to thoroughly edit and revise your manuscript. Quality should be prioritized over speed.

6. Lackluster Book Descriptions

Mistake: A boring or poorly written book description can fail to capture potential readers' interest.

Solution: Craft compelling blurbs that serve as effective advertisements for your book. Study successful descriptions in your genre for inspiration.

7. Not Establishing a Brand Identity

Mistake: Authors may overlook the importance of building a brand identity, which is crucial for gaining reader trust and recognition.

Solution: Develop a strong author brand that communicates who you are and what readers can expect from your work. This helps build a loyal audience for future publications.

By addressing these common pitfalls with proactive strategies, self-publishing authors can enhance their chances of success and reach a wider audience.

Keywords

AI agents are excellent at constructing keyword lists. In this application, I fed AI a short description of my novel Falstaff's Big Gamble and instructed it to: Generate a set of relevant keywords.

Query

In Falstaff's Big Gamble, Shakespeare's Hamlet and Othello are merged and turned into a comedy. The story takes place in Gundarland, a fantasy land, and Hamlet is a dwarf and Othello a dark elf. Falstaff is an obese human con artist who sees Hamlet and Othello as easy marks. Generate a set of relevant keywords.

Response

- *Shakespearean satire*
- *Hamlet*
- *Othello*
- *Falstaff*
- *Gundarland*
- *Fantasy comedy*
- *Dark elf*
- *Dwarf prince*
- *Absurdist farce*
- *Piracy*
- *Trolls and elves*
- *Mythical creatures*
- *Con artist*
- *Shakespearean parody*
- *Blended plotlines*
- *Denmarko*
- *Dun Hythe*
- *Chief of Homeland Security*
- *Thieves' Guild*
- *Satirical fantasy world*

An issue here is that you have to determine if any of these are too far off the mark and how many you want to use.

Optional query

You can use this one to check on an existing book.

List the keywords for {enter title}.

Book blurbs

Book blurbs are an important part of both publishing and marketing activities. Blurbs can be used as an introduction to a book's description and can be used in their entirety or in part for social media posts.

The following is a demonstration of what an AI program can do with blurbs:

Query

In Falstaff's Big Gamble, Shakespeare's Hamlet and Othello are merged and turned into a comedy. The story takes place in Gundarland, a fantasy land and Hamlet is a dwarf and Othello a dark elf. Falstaff is an obese human con artist who sees Hamlet and Othello as easy marks. Create a 50 word book blurb

Response

In Falstaff's Big Gamble, Shakespeare's iconic tragedies, Hamlet and Othello, are hilariously reimagined as a fantasy comedy in Gundarland. Hamlet is a dwarf prince, Othello a dark elf, and Falstaff an opportunistic human con artist scheming his way to power. Packed with trolls, pirates, and absurd twists, this is

Shakespeare like you've never seen before!

This is nice, but it can get better. I modified the query to tell it to use keywords.

Query

In Falstaff's Big Gamble, Shakespeare's Hamlet and Othello are merged and turned into a comedy. The story takes place in Gundarland, a fantasy land and Hamlet is a dwarf and Othello a dark elf. Falstaff is an obese human con artist who sees Hamlet and Othello as easy marks. Create a 50-word book blurb *and insert keywords where appropriate.*

Response

In Falstaff's Big Gamble, Shakespeare's <u>Hamlet</u> and <u>Othello</u> collide in <u>Gundarland</u>, a <u>comedic</u> fantasy world of dwarves, elves, and trolls. Hamlet, a dwarf prince, and Othello, <u>a dark elf</u>, are ensnared by Falstaff, a scheming human con artist. Packed with satire, <u>piracy</u>, and <u>absurd twists</u>, it's Shakespeare's worst nightmare turned hilarious adventure.

I underlined those keywords. Search engines LOVE text with keywords in it. Thus the second blurb is much more powerful that the first one.

Fiction Description

The book description is a crucial part of the marketing strategy. It's what appears on the landing page on bookseller sites (think Amazon). The description can go a long way toward convincing the reader to purchase the book.

Query

In Falstaff's Big Gamble, Shakespeare's Hamlet and Othello are merged and turned into a comedy. The story takes place in Gundarland, a fantasy land and Hamlet is a dwarf and Othello a dark elf. Falstaff is an obese human con artist who sees Hamlet and Othello as easy marks. Write a 300-word description using keywords where possible.

Response

Falstaff's Big Gamble is a whimsical reimagining of Shakespeare's Hamlet and Othello, set in the fantastical land of Gundarland. This comedic adventure transforms Hamlet into a brooding Dwarven prince and Othello into a stoic Dark Elf, while Sir John Falstaff retains his identity as a scheming, gluttonous human con artist. The novel weaves these iconic characters into a farcical plot filled with deception, piracy, and political intrigue.

The story begins with Falstaff exploiting Othello's trust by pretending to recruit forces to combat piracy in Dun Hythe, only to steal ships and embark on his own piratical ventures. Meanwhile, Hamlet grapples with his suspicions about his uncle Clodio's role in his father's death, all while contemplating an unusual career in beekeeping. Falstaff's machinations bring the two protagonists together as he manipulates their vulnerabilities for personal gain. His schemes culminate in convincing Hamlet, now king of Denmarko, to launch a preemptive strike against Dun Hythe under the guise of averting an invasion.

The novel blends Shakespearean tragedy with absurd humor, sidestepping deep character development in favor of a plot-driven narrative. Falstaff serves as the linchpin connecting Hamlet and Othello's stories, orchestrating chaos while remaining true to his original persona—a boastful rogue cloaked in false nobility. Alongside him are colorful characters like Desdemona's grandmother, the "Godmother," a crime boss whose presence adds tension and hilarity.

Hank Quense's Falstaff's Big Gamble offers a satirical take on classic literature, turning Shakespeare's "worst nightmare" into a laugh-out-loud fantasy romp. With trolls, elves, dwarves, and humans navigating comedic twists and turns, this unconventional tale invites readers—whether familiar with the Bard or not—into its quirky world of flawed heroes and cunning villains.

You can use this description as a model for your own version. You don't have to upload your entire manuscript to get useful responses. A good description or a synopsis will do the trick.

Nonfiction description

Nonfiction books need a great description just as novels do. In both cases, it's a major component on the book's landing page.

Query

My book Creating Your First Novel describes the five phases involved in creating a novel: planning, writing, publishing, marketing and author business. Write a 200-word description and insert keywords where appropriate.

Response

Creating a novel involves navigating through five crucial phases: planning, writing, publishing, marketing, and the author business. Each phase is essential to transforming an idea into a successful novel.

Planning is the foundation of novel writing. It involves developing a compelling story idea, fleshing out characters, and outlining the plot structure. This phase helps writers establish a clear direction and maintain focus throughout the writing process

During the writing phase, authors bring their stories to life. This stage requires discipline and motivation to complete the first draft. Writers often set daily word count targets and deadlines to maintain momentum. Revising and editing follow, refining the manuscript into a polished piece.

The publishing phase involves preparing the manuscript for publication. Authors must decide between traditional publishing or self-publishing routes. This step includes formatting the manuscript, designing a cover, and possibly hiring an editor to ensure quality.

Marketing is crucial for reaching readers and generating interest in the novel. Authors use various strategies, such as social media promotion, book signings, and collaborations with bloggers or influencers, to build their audience and increase sales.

Finally, the author business aspect focuses on managing finances, building a brand, and planning future projects. Successful authors treat their writing as a business, continually seeking opportunities for growth and development.

Upon examination this description may stand as is.

Book categories
Fiction book categories

In this application, I used AI to come up with an appropriate group of categories for my novel. Here I added the line: "What book categories should I use with Kindle" to my description.

Query

In Falstaff's Big Gamble, Shakespeare's Hamlet and Othello are merged and turned into a comedy. The story takes place in Gundarland, a fantasy land and Hamlet is a dwarf and Othello a dark elf. Falstaff is an obese human con artist who sees Hamlet and Othello as easy marks. What book categories should I use with Kindle?

Response

- *Fantasy*
  - *Subcategory: Humorous Fantasy*
- *Humor & Satire*
  - *Subcategory: Parody*
- *Literary Fiction*
  - *Subcategory: Adaptations or Shakespearean Fiction*
- *Fiction*
  - *Subcategory: Action & Adventure*

Categories can be tricky. There is a standard category listing you can find on the internet and then there are the Kindle listings, which are quite different. The categories Perplexity listed in its response are more akin to the standard categories rather than the Kindle ones. You'll need to match this list with the closest categories on Kindle.

Still, this is much better than trying to figure out the Kindle categories without a guide.

For a nonfiction book, you would use a similar prompt.

Phase 4: Marketing

Marketing introduction

Artificial Intelligence has the capacity to generate detailed marketing plans that can allow an author to spend more time on the actual marketing implementation. Marketing efforts can be more accurately targeted thanks to AI insights generated in response to specific queries.

Let's explore exactly what AI can do for an author looking for marketing help.

Query

My new book will be launched in a few weeks. How do I market it?

Response

Running a successful book launch event involves careful planning and execution to maximize engagement and sales. Here are some of the best strategies to consider:

Planning and Preparation

1. Set the Stage Early:

- Begin preparations at least two months in advance to ensure all details are in place by the launch day.
- Build an email list to create buzz and gather potential attendees.

2. Choose the Right Date and Venue:
- Select a date close to your book release to maintain marketing momentum.
- Consider venues that align with your book's theme, such as bookstores, cafes, or galleries.
- For virtual events, choose reliable streaming platforms like YouTube or Zoom.

Event Execution

1. Host Interactive Events:
- Organize live Q&A sessions where readers can interact directly with you.
- Conduct virtual or in-person book readings with audience participation.

2. Personal Engagement:
- Deliver a memorable speech that shares personal stories and insights into your writing process.
- Engage attendees personally to make them feel part of your narrative.

3. Offer Special Promotions:
- Introduce launch price offers or bundled

deals with previous works to attract buyer.

- *Host giveaways or contests to generate excitement and engagement.*

Post-Launch Activities

1. *Gather Feedback:*
- *Use feedback from the event to improve future launches and engage with your audience post-launch.*
2. *Build a Community:*
- *Foster a sense of community among attendees by creating private groups or offering exclusive content.*

By implementing these strategies, you can create a memorable and successful book launch event that not only promotes your book but also builds a lasting connection with your readers.

Strategic marketing

Your strategic marketing plan is an essential element of your overall marketing strategy. A well-crafted plan serves as a roadmap for your marketing efforts, aligning them with your business goals and target audience. It typically

includes:
1. Market analysis
2. Target audience definition
3. Competitive positioning
4. Marketing objectives
5. Marketing mix strategies (product, price, place, promotion)
6. Budget allocation
7. Implementation timeline
8. Performance metrics and evaluation methods

By developing and following a strategic marketing plan, you can ensure more effective resource allocation, improved decision-making, and better overall marketing performance.

Query

Why is a strategic marketing plan so important for book marketing?

Response

A strategic marketing plan is crucial for book marketing due to several key reasons:

1. Increased Visibility and Reach

A well-crafted marketing plan significantly boosts the visibility of a book in a crowded market. With millions of books published annually, a strategic approach helps ensure that the book reaches its target audience through various channels such as social media, email marketing, and advertising. This increased visibility is essential for standing out among numerous competitors.

2. Building Buzz and Engagement

Strategic marketing helps generate excitement and anticipation around a book. This can be achieved through tactics like book launch events, signings, giveaways, and influencer reviews. Creating buzz not only attracts readers but also encourages word-of-mouth promotion, which is invaluable for building a loyal readership.

3. Understanding and Targeting the Audience

A strategic plan involves thorough market research to understand the target audience's preferences and behaviors. By analyzing metrics and engagement data, authors can tailor their marketing efforts to better meet the needs of their audience, leading to higher conversion rates and more effective outreach.

4. Proactive Marketing Approach

Having a strategic plan allows authors to be proactive rather than reactive in their marketing efforts. Instead of waiting for readers to discover their book, authors can actively promote it to the right audience. This approach maximizes exposure and increases the chances of achieving bestseller status.

5. Establishing a Strong Author Brand

A strategic marketing plan helps in building an attractive author brand that fosters relationships with readers and booksellers. A cohesive brand not only aids in selling more books but also converts one-time buyers into lifelong fans by creating engaging and relatable messaging.

6. Flexibility and Adaptation

A marketing strategy is not static; it allows for flexibility and adaptation based on ongoing data analysis and feedback from readers and industry professionals. This adaptability ensures that marketing efforts remain aligned with audience preferences and market trends, enhancing overall effectiveness.

In summary, a strategic marketing plan is indispensable for successfully promoting a book. It provides a roadmap for increasing visibility, engaging with audiences, understanding market dynamics, and building a strong author brand—all essential components for achieving success in the competitive publishing landscape.

Fiction book strategic plan

Let's use AI to come up with a plan for a novel

Query

Develop a strategic marketing plan for my humorous fantasy novel

Response

Developing a strategic marketing plan for your humorous fantasy novel involves several key steps to ensure your book reaches its target audience and achieves the desired sales and recognition. Here's a structured approach based on the search results:

Develop Your Strategy

1. Define Your Target Audience:

- *Identify the demographic most likely to enjoy your humorous fantasy novel. Consider age, interests, and reading habits.*
- *Engage with online communities that focus on fantasy and humor to understand their preferences.*

2. Set Clear Goals:

- *Establish specific objectives such as gaining exposure, increasing sales, or building a fan base.*

- *Consider goals like landing on bestseller lists or generating local interest.*

3. Budget Planning:

- *Determine how much you are willing to spend on marketing efforts, including ads, promotions, and events.*

Choose Your Tactics

1. Book Cover and Blurb:

- *Invest in a professional book cover that reflects the humor and fantasy elements of your novel.*

- *Write a compelling blurb that captures the essence of your story and hooks potential readers.*

2. Social Media Marketing:

- *Use platforms like Instagram, TikTok, and Twitter to share engaging content related to your book's themes, characters, and settings.*

- *Create content such as memes, quotes, and videos that highlight the humorous aspects of your novel.*

3. Networking and Reviews:

- *Connect with book reviewers and influencers in the fantasy genre to gain reviews and endorsements.*

- *Consider sending promotional boxes with*

your book and themed swag to encourage social media sharing.

4. Advertisements:

- *Utilize platforms like Facebook and Amazon for targeted ads that reach fantasy readers.*
- *Analyze which ads perform best and adjust your strategy accordingly.*

5. Blog Tours and Guest Posts:

- *Participate in blog tours related to fantasy literature to increase visibility.*
- *Write guest posts for relevant blogs to reach new audiences without overtly selling your book.*

Create Your Timeline

1. *Planning Phase:*

- *Draft a comprehensive marketing plan that aligns with your book's release schedule.*
- *Prepare all necessary materials such as press releases, cover reveals, and social media content.*

2. *Pre-Order Campaign:*

- *Build anticipation by offering pre-order incentives such as exclusive content or discounts.*
- *Engage with your audience through newsletters and social media updates*

leading up to the launch.

3. Post-Release Activities:

- *Continue promoting your book through regular social media posts, email newsletters, and community engagement.*
- *Plan ongoing activities like giveaways or special promotions to sustain interest over time.*

By following these steps, you can create a strategic marketing plan tailored specifically for your humorous fantasy novel, maximizing its potential for success in the market.

This response is rather generic because I didn't provide much detail in the initial query. If you provide more detailed information in the query, the response will be more reflective of your situation rather than the generic version you have here.

Nonfiction book strategic marketing plan

Now we'll use AI to put together a plan for a nonfiction book. The query will reference the book you are now reading. This query has more details about the book.

Query

Develop a strategic marketing plan for my new nonfiction book on how writers can utilize AI programs.

Response

Strategic Marketing Plan for Your Nonfiction Book on AI for Writers

To effectively market your new nonfiction book on how writers can utilize AI programs, a comprehensive and strategic marketing plan is essential. This plan will leverage traditional and AI-driven marketing strategies to reach your target audience, maximize visibility, and drive sales.

1. Identify Your Target Audience

Understanding your target audience is crucial. Consider the demographics, interests, and preferred platforms of potential readers. For a book on AI for writers, your audience might include professional writers, aspiring authors, tech enthusiasts, and educators interested in integrating AI into writing processes.

2. Develop a Unique Selling Proposition (USP)

Clearly define what makes your book unique. Highlight the benefits of using AI in writing and how your book provides practical insights or tools that are not available elsewhere. This USP will be central to all marketing materials.

3. Leverage AI-Driven Marketing Tools

- *Utilize AI tools to enhance your marketing strategy:*
- *Personalization: Use AI to create personalized marketing campaigns that resonate with specific reader segments.*
- *Data Analytics: Employ AI to analyze market trends and reader preferences, enabling more effective targeting.*
- *Social Media Optimization: Use AI to determine the best times to post and the most engaging content types for your audience.*

4. Build an Online Presence

A strong online presence is vital:

- *Website and Blog: Create a website or blog dedicated to your book where you can share insights, updates, and engage with readers.*
- *Social Media: Regularly post engaging content on platforms like Twitter, Instagram, and LinkedIn. Consider sharing excerpts or creating a Twitter thread of key chapters to generate interest.*

- *Email Marketing: Build an email list to send newsletters with exclusive content or updates about your book.*

5. Engage with Readers and Influencers

Engagement is key to building a community around your book:

- *Reviews and Testimonials: Encourage early readers to leave reviews on platforms like Amazon and Goodreads.*
- *Influencer Collaborations: Use AI tools to identify influencers who align with your book's theme and collaborate with them for promotions.*
- *Interactive Elements: Consider adding interactive elements within the book or creating a companion app that enhances reader engagement.*

6. Utilize Traditional Marketing Channels

Don't overlook traditional marketing methods:

- *Book Launch Events: Host virtual or physical launch events to generate buzz.*
- *Press Releases and Media Outreach: Send press releases to relevant media outlets and participate in interviews or podcasts for additional exposure.*

- *Collaborations with Other Authors: Partner with authors in similar genres for joint promotions or events.*

7. Monitor and Adjust Your Strategy

Use analytics tools to track the performance of your marketing efforts:

- *Regularly review data from social media, website traffic, and sales metrics.*
- *Adjust strategies based on what is working best to optimize results over time.*

By integrating these strategies into your marketing plan, you can effectively promote your nonfiction book on utilizing AI programs for writers, ensuring it reaches the right audience and achieves its sales goals.

As you can see, adding more specific information in the query allows AI to provide a more focused response. This response can now serve as the strategic marketing plan for this book and will be used to market it.

In the fiction query, I only said "humorous fantasy." In this query, I said, "nonfiction book on how writers can utilize AI programs." You can see the differences in the details of the responses.

Marketing plans

Now let's turn to using AI to develop a marketing plan for your new book. We authors can always use help with the marketing aspects. This next query is a variation of the query I used in the first section of this chapter. The response is somewhat different, and this query demonstrates your options on how to use the AI program.

Query

My new book will be launched on March 1. Prepare a six-week launch marketing plan for this event starting two weeks before launch.

Response

Six-Week Book Launch Marketing Plan

Below is a detailed marketing plan for your book launch event on March 1, starting two weeks before the launch and continuing four weeks after.

Two weeks to Launch Day (Pre-Launch Phase)

1. Build Anticipation

Social Media Campaigns:

- *Share teasers, snippets, and behind-the-scenes content about the book on platforms like Instagram, Facebook, and Twitter.*
- *Post a countdown to launch day with*

engaging visuals and hashtags relevant to your book's genre.

Pre-Orders:

- *Set up pre-orders on platforms like Amazon and incentivize them with exclusive bonuses (e.g., signed copies, access to a live Q&A.*

Email Marketing:

- *Launch an email campaign to your subscribers, starting with an announcement about the book and following up with sneak peeks, testimonials, and countdown emails.*

Influencer Outreach:

- *Partner with influencers or bloggers in your niche to promote early reviews or features of your book.*

2. Media and PR

- *Distribute press releases to relevant media outlets about your upcoming book launch.*
- *Schedule interviews or guest appearances on podcasts or blogs related to your book's theme.*

Launch Week (March 1)

1. Celebrate the Launch

- *Host a virtual or in-person launch party. Include a reading session, Q&A, and giveaways for attendees.*

- *Announce the launch across all social media platforms with compelling visuals and direct links to purchase the book.*

2. Promotional Offers

- *Offer limited-time deals such as discounted eBook prices (e.g., $0.99) during launch week to boost sales.*
- *Run ads on platforms like Facebook, Amazon, or BookBub targeting your audience demographics.*

3. Engage Your Audience

- *Respond actively to comments, messages, and reviews on social media.*
- *Share user-generated content such as photos of readers with your book or their review.*

Weeks +1 to +4 (Post-Launch Phase

1. Maintain Momentum

- *Continue posting engaging content on social media, such as reader testimonials, excerpts from reviews, or polls about favorite parts of the book.*
- *Host live sessions discussing themes in your book or your writing journey.*

2. Expand Reach

- *Organize a virtual blog tour by guest-posting on blogs within your niche.*

- *Appear as a guest on podcasts or YouTube channels that cater to your target audience.*
- ***3 Encourage readers who purchased the book to leave reviews on Amazon, Goodreads, or other platforms****.*
- *Highlight positive reviews in your marketing materials.*
  4. **Cross-Promotions**
- *Promote any backlist titles if applicable or collaborate with other authors for joint promotions.*

This plan ensures consistent engagement before, during, and after the launch while leveraging multiple channels to maximize visibility and sales.

You are probably amazed — as I was — at the depth and completeness of the response. It contains a few items that I won't do, like hosting live sessions on the theses in the book. You too may have to cut the list down a bit. Still, this is a great start to launching your new book.

Press release

AI can be a great help when it comes to creating a press release. Let's see just how great it is.

Query

In Falstaff's Big Gamble, Shakespeare's Hamlet and Othello are merged and turned into a comedy. The story takes place in Gundarland, a fantasy land and Hamlet is a dwarf and Othello a dark elf. Falstaff is an obese human con artist who sees Hamlet and Othello as easy marks. Write a press release using keywords where possible.

Response

Press Release: Dive into the Hilarious World of "Falstaff's Big Gamble"

Step into Gundarland, a fantastical realm brimming with dwarves, elves, and humans, where Shakespeare's greatest tragedies are hilariously transformed into a riotous comedy! Hank Quense's *Falstaff's Big Gamble* is a bold reimagining of *Hamlet* and *Othello*, merging these iconic tales into a single comedic adventure unlike anything you've read before.

A Shakespearean Mash-Up in Fantasy Form

In this uproarious parody, Hamlet is no

longer the brooding Danish prince but a dwarf torn between his passion for beekeeping and avenging his father's murder. Othello is reimagined as a dark elf grappling with his duties as the Minister of Homeland Security in the bustling city of Dun Hythe. At the heart of the chaos is Falstaff, Shakespeare's infamous rogue, now an obese human con artist who sees both Hamlet and Othello as easy marks for his schemes.

A Plot Full of Twists and Laughs

Falstaff's antics lead to outrageous situations—from convincing Othello to fund a pirate-hunting force (only to become a pirate himself) to meddling in Hamlet's quest for vengeance. With witty dialogue, clever satire, and unexpected plot twists, *Falstaff's Big Gamble* offers a fresh take on Shakespeare's timeless characters while delivering laugh-out-loud moments.

Why Readers Love It

- Accessible Humor: You don't need to be a Shakespeare aficionado to enjoy this comedic masterpiece.
- Unique Setting: Gundarland is a vibrant fantasy world filled with diverse races like dwarves, elves, and yuks, all living together amidst humorous conflicts.

- *Memorable Characters: From Hamlet's bee obsession to Falstaff's scheming brilliance, every character shines in this unconventional tale.*

Praise for Hank Quense

Critics and readers alike have hailed Quense as a master of humor and satire. His ability to blend Shakespearean elements with fantasy tropes creates an unforgettable reading experience.

Available Now!

*Don't miss your chance to explore Gundarland and witness Shakespeare's worst nightmare turned into comedic gold. *Falstaff's Big Gamble* is available in eBook format.*

Grab your copy today and prepare for an adventure filled with laughter, piracy, politics, and bees!

I would use this one just the way it is. No changes required

Targeting-1

Targeting is a marketing essential, but many authors don't understand it or chose to ignore it. The reality is that the vast majority of the general population is not interested in your book. Spending money on an ad aimed at the general population is often a waste of money. To be successful, an ad or promotion must be targeted to the specific segment of the general population that is interested in your genre.

Let's explore how AI can help with this challenge.

General query: How can I reach my targeted audience for my {insert here} novel?

Query

How can I reach my targeted audience for my fantasy novel?

Response

To effectively reach your target audience for a fantasy novel, consider the following strategies:

Identify Your Target Audience

1. Understand Your Genre: Clearly define your novel's genre and subgenre to identify the specific audience interested in such stories. For example, if your book is a young adult fantasy, your target audience will likely be teenagers aged 13-18 who enjoy magic and adventure.

2. Create a Reader Profile: Develop a detailed profile of your ideal reader, including demographics, interests, and reading habits.

Consider their age, favorite genres, and the platforms they frequent for book recommendations.

3. Research Reader Preferences: Use platforms like Goodreads and Reddit to explore what readers in your genre are discussing. Identify common themes or elements they enjoy in fantasy novels and incorporate these into your marketing strategy.

Marketing Strategies

1. Book Cover and Launch: Ensure your book cover is attractive and fits the subgenre to capture potential readers' attention. A successful launch can significantly impact your book's discoverability.

2. Social Media Engagement: Use social media platforms like Instagram, TikTok, and Facebook to share content related to your book's setting, characters, themes, and more. Engage with followers by posting consistently about these elements rather than just promoting sales.

3. Networking with Book Reviewers: Connect with book reviewers who specialize in fantasy genres. Send them promotional materials or "promotional boxes" to increase their interest in sharing your book with their audience.

4. Advertising: Utilize targeted ads on platforms like Facebook and Amazon that cater to fantasy readers. Monitor the performance of these ads to optimize your strategy.

5. Email Newsletters: Build an email list to maintain direct contact with interested readers. This allows you to own your audience's contact information and communicate directly with them about new releases or updates.

6. Collaborations and Guest Posts: Write guest posts on related blogs or collaborate with other authors in your genre to expand your reach.

By understanding your target audience and employing these marketing strategies, you can effectively reach and engage potential readers for your fantasy novel.

While it has a lot of material in it, I think this response is rather bland and generic. I think AI can do better with a different query.

Targeting-2

Let's try this query and see what happens.
Query

My novel is a fantasy story. How can I reach fantasy readers rather than the general population?

Response

To effectively reach fantasy readers rather than the general population, consider the following strategies:

Understand Your Audience

- *Identify Reader Preferences: Understand what elements fantasy readers are drawn to, such as specific creatures, themes, or settings. Engage with platforms like Reddit (e.g., r/fantasy) to research reader preferences and trends.*
- *Target Specific Subgenres: Different subgenres of fantasy (e.g., high fantasy, urban fantasy) attract different audiences. Tailor your marketing efforts to align with the specific interests of your target subgenre.*

Initial Marketing Strategies

- *Book Cover Design: Ensure your book cover is appealing and genre-appropriate. A well-designed cover can significantly impact a reader's decision to pick up your book.*
- *Pre-Order Campaigns: Set up pre-order campaigns to generate early interest and*

reviews. This can help create momentum for your book launch.

Ongoing Marketing Strategies

- *Social Media Engagement: Use social media platforms effectively by focusing on the content within your book rather than just promoting its availability. Highlight unique elements like characters, themes, and settings.*
- *Advertising: Consider using targeted ads on platforms like Facebook and Amazon, which have been effective for fantasy books. Analyze which platforms work best for your specific type of fantasy.*

Community Building

- *Join Online Communities: Engage with online communities such as Goodreads and fantasy-specific forums to connect with potential readers and gather feedback.*
- *Collaborate with Other Authors: Network with authors in the same genre to cross-promote each other's work. This can expand your reach within the fantasy community.*

Additional Tips

- *Newsletter Campaigns: Build an email list to maintain direct contact with your*

*audience. Use newsletters to share
updates, exclusive content, and
promotions.*
- *Market Research: Continuously research
your audience using tools like Goodreads
reviews and social media insights to
refine your marketing strategy.*

*By focusing on these targeted strategies,
you can more effectively reach and engage
with fantasy readers who are most likely to
appreciate your novel.*

This response is better in my opinion. It has
more specific ideas and comments.

Hashtags

In this query, I requested AI to come up
with hashtags. Hashtags are useful for adding
posts to social media sites.

Query

In Falstaff's Big Gamble, Shakespeare's
Hamlet and Othello are merged and turned into
a comedy. The story takes place in
Gundarland, a fantasy land and Hamlet is a
dwarf and Othello a dark elf. Falstaff is an

obese human con artist who sees Hamlet and Othello as easy marks. Generate a list of appropriate hashtags.

Response

Here is a list of appropriate hashtags for "Falstaff's Big Gamble":

#FalstaffsBigGamble

#ShakespeareComedy

#FantasyRetelling

#HamletDwarf

#OthelloDarkElf

#Gundarland

#ShakespeareParody

#FantasyComedy

#FalstaffTheConman

#ShakespeareanHumor

A query like this takes the work out of developing a list by yourself.

Fiction social media posts

This query is a biggie. AI can really shine in this endeavor. Let's ask it to create five posts for X (or Twitter)

Here's the general form of the query: Based on the following storyline {Insert storyline} write 5 social media posts for {insert social media platform}.

Query

In Falstaff's Big Gamble, Shakespeare's Hamlet and Othello are merged and turned into a comedy. The story takes place in Gundarland, a fantasy land and Hamlet is a dwarf and Othello a dark elf. Falstaff is an obese human con artist who sees Hamlet and Othello as easy marks. Write 5 social media posts for X.

Response

Here are five social media posts for X about the comedic story set in Gundarland:

1. Welcome to Gundarland! Where a sneeze from an omniscient god created a world of hilarity! Meet Hamlet, a dwarf with a flair for drama, and Othello, a dark elf with a penchant for intrigue. Together, they navigate this whimsical land where laughter is the best magic! #GundarlandAdventures #FantasyFun

2. Falstaff's New Con! In Gundarland, Falstaff isn't just any con artist; he's an obese human with a knack for spotting easy marks like Hamlet and Othello. Will his schemes succeed, or will he end up in more trouble than he bargained for? Find out in this comedic twist on classic tales! #FalstaffFails #ComedyGold

3. Dwarfs, Elves, and Hijinks! 🐾🧙 Dive into the world of Gundarland where dwarfs like Hamlet and dark elves like Othello live cheek by jowl amidst magical chaos and comedic capers. It's Shakespeare meets slapstick in this hilarious fantasy romp! #ShakespeareSpoof #FantasyLaughs

4. A Tale of Two Marks! 🙊 Falstaff sees opportunity in every corner of Gundarland, especially when it involves our unlikely heroes, Hamlet the dwarf and Othello the dark elf. Will his cons bring him riches or just more laughs? Discover the hilarity that ensues! #ConArtistChronicles #GundarlandGiggles

5. Magic, Mischief, and Mayhem! ✏️ In the land of Gundarland, nothing is as it seems. Join Hamlet, Othello, and the ever-scheming Falstaff on a journey filled with magical mishaps and laugh-out-loud moments. This is fantasy like you've never seen before! #MagicalMishaps #FantasyComedy

These posts even come with emojis and hashtags! They are ready to get a quick edit, if necessary, and to get pasted into X. You can specify other social media venues such as

LinkedIn or Facebook, and this query works just as well on nonfiction books as you see in the next section.

Nonfiction social media posts

Let's try that with a nonfiction query and Facebook.

Query

My Creating Your First Novel is a nonfiction book that describes and explains the five phases of creating a book: planning, writing, publishing, marketing and author business. Write 5 social media posts for Facebook.

Response

Here are five engaging and creative Facebook posts to promote your nonfiction book, *Creating Your First Novel*. Each post is designed to highlight the value of your book while connecting with aspiring authors.

Post 1: Inspire Aspiring Authors

Have you ever dreamed of writing your own novel but don't know where to start?

Writing a book can feel overwhelming, but it doesn't have to be! In my book, Creating Your First Novel, I break the process down into 5 clear phases:

📌 Planning

📌 Writing

📌 Publishing

📌 Marketing

📌 Building Your Author Business

Whether you're just starting out or ready to take your writing to the next level, this guide will help you every step of the way.

👉 Ready to turn your dream into reality? Grab your copy today and start creating YOUR first novel!

#AspiringAuthors #WritingTips #CreatingYourFirstNovel

Post 2: Highlight the Planning Phase

🎯 Great novels don't just happen—they're planned! 🎯

The first phase of creating a book is Planning, and it's where the magic begins. In Creating Your First Novel, I'll show you how to:

☑️ Develop your story idea

☑️ Create compelling characters

☑️ Outline your plot like a pro

If you've been staring at a blank page, this is the roadmap you need to get started.

📖 Ready to plan YOUR masterpiece? Check out my book today!

#WritingJourney #NovelPlanning #AuthorLife

Post 3: Share a Writing Tip

✎ *Struggling to stay motivated while writing?* Here's a tip from my book, Creating Your First Novel:

Set small, achievable daily goals. Whether it's 300 words or 30 minutes of writing, consistency is key.

In the Writing phase of my book, I share practical strategies like this to help you stay on track and finish your manuscript.

What's YOUR biggest writing challenge? Share in the comments—I'd love to help!

#WritingMotivation #CreatingYourFirstNovel #WritersCommunity

Post 4: Focus on Publishing

📚 Publishing your book doesn't have to be intimidating! 📚

In Creating Your First Novel, I demystify the Publishing phase by breaking down:

✔️ Traditional publishing vs. self-publishing

✔️ How to format your manuscript for

success

✔️ Tips for finding an agent or publishing on platforms like Amazon

Your story deserves to be shared with the world—let me show you how!

📖 Get your copy of Creating Your First Novel and take the next step toward becoming a published author.

#PublishingTips #SelfPublishing #AuthorGoals

Post 5: Build Excitement Around Marketing & Author Business

🚀 Did you know that writing a book is just the beginning? 🚀

Once your novel is complete, it's time to market it and build your author brand! In Creating Your First Novel, I'll teach you how to:

📢 Promote your book online and offline

💻 Use social media effectively as an author

💼 Turn your passion for writing into a thriving business

Your journey as an author doesn't end with publishing—it's just getting started! Let me guide you through every step.

Ready to create YOUR first novel AND launch your career as an author? Grab your copy today!

#BookMarketing #AuthorBusiness #CreatingYourFirstNovel

These posts are designed to be engaging and actionable while showcasing the value of your book. You can also include visuals such as an image of your book cover, a behind-the-scenes photo of you writing, or quotes from the book to make them even more appealing!

I don't have anything to add to this response that I haven't already said. Ensure the response accurately portrays your book.

Optional query

Write 5 satiric Facebook posts on {enter subject}.

Blog posts

Another use for an AI app is generating content for blog posts. Let's explore this application and see what results we can achieve.

General query form: {insert storyline} write {insert length} blog post using keywords.

Query:

In Falstaff's Big Gamble, Shakespeare's Hamlet and Othello are merged and turned into a comedy. The story takes place in Gundarland, a fantasy land and Hamlet is a dwarf and Othello a dark elf. Falstaff is an obese human con artist who sees Hamlet and Othello as easy marks. Write a 150-word blog post using keywords.

Response

In "Falstaff's Big Gamble," Hank Quense brilliantly transforms Shakespeare's iconic tragedies, Hamlet and Othello, into a comedic fantasy set in the whimsical world of Gundarland. This imaginative tale reimagines Hamlet as a dwarf prince and Othello as a dark elf, both entangled in the schemes of the notorious con artist, Falstaff. Falstaff, an obese human with a penchant for deception, sees these characters as easy targets for his cunning plans.

The story unfolds with Hamlet, the Prince of Denmarko, torn between avenging his father's murder and pursuing his dream of starting a bee-keeping business. Meanwhile, Othello is convinced by Falstaff to fund a pirate-hunting mission, only to be duped as Falstaff turns pirate himself. This plot-driven farce is filled with humor and satire, offering a fresh take on Shakespeare's works without requiring prior knowledge of the Bard's plays. With its unique setting and character dynamics, "Falstaff's Big Gamble" promises laughter and adventure in a land where dwarves, elves, and humans coexist amidst comedic chaos.

This one looks ready-to-go without any editing or rewriting.

Nonfiction trailer

For a nonfiction book, you can get AI to create a script for a trailer. Perplexity.AI doesn't have the capability to create graphics but it can write scripts.

Query

My *Creating Your First Novel* is a nonfiction book that describes and explains the five phases of creating a book: planning, writing, publishing, marketing and author business. Create a script for a seven-slide trailer.

Response

Here is a seven-slide script for the trailer of *Creating Your First Novel*, focusing on its five phases: planning, writing, publishing, marketing, and the author business.

Slide 1: Opening Hook

- Visuals: A blank notebook on a desk, a pen poised above it. The background fades into a bookshelf filled with novels.
- Text: "Every great novel starts with a single idea. But how do you turn that idea into a book?"
- Voiceover: "Discover the five essential phases to create your first novel."

Slide 2: Phase 1 - Planning

- Visuals: A writer brainstorming ideas, creating a mind map, and outlining on a whiteboard.
- Text: "Phase 1: Planning – Build the foundation of your story."
- Voiceover: "Learn how to develop your story idea, craft characters, and outline your plot for success."

Slide 3: Phase 2 - Writing

- Visuals: A writer typing furiously on a laptop, surrounded by coffee cups and crumpled paper.
- Text: "Phase 2: Writing – Bring your story to life."

- *Voiceover: "Write with abandon. Overcome self-doubt and complete your first draft."*

Slide 4: Phase 3 - Publishing

- *Visuals: A manuscript being formatted and printed, followed by stacks of books.*
- *Text: "Phase 3: Publishing – Share your story with the world."*
- *Voiceover: "Understand the paths to publishing—traditional or self-publishing —and prepare your manuscript for readers."*

Slide 5: Phase 4 - Marketing

- *Visuals: Social media posts promoting a book, book signings, and an author engaging with readers online.*
- *Text: "Phase 4: Marketing – Find your audience."*
- *Voiceover: "Master strategies to promote your novel and connect with readers globally."*

Slide 6: Phase 5 - Author Business

- *Visuals: A writer at a desk managing royalties and planning future projects.*
- *Text: "Phase 5: Author Business – Build your career as an author."*
- *Voiceover: "Learn how to manage finances, grow your brand, and plan for*

long-term success."

Slide 7: Closing Call-to-Action

- *Visuals: The book cover of *Creating Your First Novel* appears on screen alongside glowing reviews.*
- *Text: "Your journey begins here. Get your copy today!"*
- *Voiceover: "Start turning your dream of writing a novel into reality. Order now!"*

This trailer script highlights the inspiring and practical approach of the book while enticing viewers to embark on their writing journey.

This response can be used as a starting point to create slides that can later be turned into a complete video. There are several tools available to do this, including Powerpoint or Keywords and websites like Canva.

However, trying to get an AI to write a script for a novel is quite a different story. AI suggested visuals of the characters using dialog to make points about the story. I judged this approach to be less than optimal and too difficult to attempt unless I had access to a recording studio, which would be necessary for creating high-quality character dialogue.

Phase 5: Author business

Whether you know it or not, whether you want this to happen or not, as soon as you publish a book, you essentially own a company. You are the CEO! The purpose of this new venture is to market and sell your book.

There are several reasons why you need to take this seriously. One reason is taxes. Royalties are taxable income. If you operate as a company, the tax authorities will allow you to deduct book-related expenses from the royalties. If the tax authorities believe your writing is a hobby, not a business, they will limit the deductions.

A second reason is that thinking of yourself as a CEO will force you to approach your work like a business owner, and your decisions will be based on business needs, not your ego. I can't stress enough how important this point is.

What do new authors overlook when it comes to business?

In this first query for this phase, I'll ask Ai to provide a list of common mistakes or stuff that authors tend to overlook at first.

Query

What do new authors overlook when it comes to business?

Response

New authors often overlook several crucial aspects of the business side of writing, which can significantly impact their success. Here are some common oversights:

Market Research and Target Audience

- *Lack of Market Research: New authors frequently fail to research their target market thoroughly. Understanding what readers want and identifying current trends is essential for aligning their work with market demands.*
- *Target Audience Misalignment: Authors may not clearly define their target audience, leading to marketing efforts that don't effectively reach potential readers.*

Publishing Knowledge

- *Insufficient Knowledge of the Publishing Process**: Many new authors are unfamiliar with the intricacies of publishing, whether traditional or self-publishing. This lack of knowledge can lead to unrealistic expectations and poor decision-making.*
- *Ignoring Industry Trends: Authors who do not keep up with industry trends may miss opportunities for innovation or fall victim to outdated practices.*

Business and Financial Planning

- *Neglecting Business Aspects: Viewing writing solely as an art form can result in neglecting essential business practices like financial planning, tax considerations, and paperwork management.*
- *No Business Plan: Without a clear business plan, authors may struggle to set realistic goals and measure progress effectively.*

Marketing and Branding

- *Underestimating Marketing Needs: New authors often delay marketing efforts until after publication, missing out on building pre-launch buzz and failing to establish a strong author brand.*

- *Weak Online Presence: A lack of a professional online presence, such as an author website or active social media profiles, can limit an author's ability to connect with readers and promote their work effectively.*

Networking and Community Building

- *Limited Networking Efforts: Building relationships with other authors, publishers, and industry professionals is crucial for gaining support and opening new opportunities. New authors may not prioritize networking sufficiently.*
- *Engagement with Readers: Fostering a community among readers through newsletters, social media interactions, and feedback loops is often overlooked but is vital for building a loyal fan base.*

By addressing these common oversights, new authors can better navigate the business aspects of writing, enhancing their chances of success in the competitive literary market.

The bullet items under **Business and Financial Planning** are the themes of this phase in the book.

Breaking even

When you are publishing a book, you incur expenses. A logical business question is this: At what point will my royalties equal my expenses? In other words, when I will break even? Let's see what AI says about this.

Query

How will I know when my book royalties will equal or exceed my expenses?

Response

To determine when your book royalties will equal or exceed your expenses, you need to follow these steps:

1. Calculate Your Royalties

First, understand how your royalties are calculated. Royalties can be based on either the retail price or net sales of your book:

- *Retail Price Royalties: Typically, royalties are a percentage of the retail price of the book. For example, if your book retails at $20 and your royalty rate is 5%, you earn $1 per book sold.*
- *Net Sales Royalties: These are calculated after discounts and other deductions. This method can result in higher percentages but is based on the net amount received by the publisher.*

2. Determine Your Expenses

Identify all costs associated with publishing and marketing your book. These might include:

- *Production Costs: Printing, cover design, editing, etc.*
- *Marketing and Distribution Costs: Advertising, distribution fees, shipping, etc.*
- *Miscellaneous Costs: Any other expenses incurred during the process.*

3. Calculate Break-Even Point

To find out when your royalties will equal or exceed your expenses, calculate the break-even point:

Break-even Point (in units) = Total Expenses\Royalty per Book

For example, if your total expenses are $5,000 and you earn $1 per book sold in royalties, you would need to sell 5,000 books to break even.

4. Monitor Sales and Adjust

Use tools such as royalty management software to track sales and expenses efficiently. These tools can help you see real-time data on sales performance and profitability.

By understanding these calculations and using available tools to track progress, you can determine when your book royalties will match or surpass your expenses.

I found this response to be incomplete. The analysis applies only to print book sales distributed by a publishing house and doesn't address the more complex scenario required for self-publishing authors. This limited answer is the result of insufficient information provided in the query. I didn't tell AI the royalties are from a self-published book. This response brings up two important facts about AI programs: First, queries will be literally interpreted by AI and second, don't accept responses as infallible.

To get a more comprehensive response, let's modify the query and see what happens.

Query

How will I know when my self-published book royalties will equal or exceed my expenses?

Response

*To determine when your self-published book royalties will equal or exceed your expenses, you need to calculate your **break-even point**. This involves understanding your total expenses, per-unit earnings (royalties), and the number of books you need to sell to* cover those costs.

Steps to Calculate When Royalties Will Cover Expenses

1. Calculate Total Expenses

Your total expenses include all costs associated with self-publishing, such as:

- Editing and formatting: Costs vary based on book length and quality but are often indispensable.
- Cover design: Can range from $50 for basic designs to $1,000+ for professional work.
- Printing costs: For physical books, printing costs depend on size, page count, and print method (e.g., print-on-demand or bulk printing). Print-on-demand typically costs $0.50–$1.50 per book.
- Marketing and promotion: Optional but impactful; expenses may include ads, website development, or social media campaigns.
- Publishing platform fees: Some platforms charge setup fees or take a percentage of sales.

For example, if you spend $500 on editing, $300 on cover design, and $200 on marketing, your total expenses are $1,000.

2. Determine Per-Book Royalty Earnings

The royalty per book depends on:

- *The platform (e.g., Amazon KDP, Draft2Digital).*
- *The book's price and royalty rate.*

For instance:

- *Amazon KDP offers 70% royalties for ebooks priced between $2.99 and $9.99, minus a delivery fee.*
- *If your ebook is priced at $4.99 with a 70% royalty rate and a $0.10 delivery fee, you earn approximately $3.39 per sale.*

For print books:

- *Royalties are calculated after deducting printing and distribution costs. If your print book retails for $15 and printing/ distribution costs are $7, you earn $8 per sale.*

3. Calculate the Break-Even Point

Use the formula:

Break-even sales = Total Expenses\Per-book Royalty

For example:

If your total expenses are $1,000 and you earn $3.39 per ebook sale:

Break-even sales = 1000/3.39 = approx

295 books

This means you need to sell approximately 295 ebooks to cover your expenses.

4. Track Sales and Adjust

Use tools like ScribeCount or PublishWide to track royalties across platforms and monitor progress toward profitability. These tools help consolidate data from multiple marketplaces and provide insights into profitability by factoring in sales and advertising expenses.

5. Consider Tax Deductions

As a self-published author, you may qualify for tax deductions on expenses like editing services, marketing costs, or home office use. These deductions can reduce your overall financial burden.

6. Monitor Marketing ROI

If you're spending on ads or promotions, track their return on investment (ROI). Tools like PublishWide allow you to compare ad performance against royalties earned to ensure you're not overspending.

By carefully calculating expenses and monitoring sales data, you'll know exactly when your royalties equal or exceed your publishing costs.

This response is much better. It also illustrates the danger of not writing a query correctly. In this case, the addition of a single word drastically changed the AI response.

Business problems

In this instance, AI can help you solve a problem.

The general query format looks like this: I'm having trouble with {insert issue}. Provide a detailed list of ways to {fix/solve/eliminate} this issue with specific details.

It's important that you provide enough details about the issue so AI knows exactly what problem to address. You may need to reissue the query several times before AI provides a solution for correct issue.

I'll use a basic business query as an example.

Query

I just self-published my first book, and I'm wondering if I should start a business. What do you advise?

Response

Deciding whether to start a business after self-publishing your first book depends on your goals, resources, and long-term vision. Here are some key considerations and advice to help you make an informed decision:

Why Start a Business?

Starting a business for your self-publishing endeavors can provide several benefits:

- *Professional Branding: Operating under a business name (e.g., an LLC) can enhance your credibility as an author and publisher. It also helps establish a professional image, especially if you plan to expand into other ventures like publishing additional books, offering courses, or consulting.*
- *Tax Advantages: A formal business structure can offer tax benefits, such as deducting expenses related to publishing, marketing, and operations.*
- *Legal Protection: Forming a legal entity (like an LLC) separates your personal assets from your business liabilities, offering protection if any legal issues arise.*
- *Creative Control: Owning a publishing company allows you to control every aspect of the process, from design to marketing strategies, without being dependent on third parties.*

Challenges of Starting a Business

While there are benefits, starting a business also comes with challenges:

- Time and Effort: Running a business requires time for administrative tasks like bookkeeping, marketing, and managing operations. This could detract from writing or other creative pursuits.
- Financial Investment: Setting up a business involves costs such as registration fees, hiring professionals (editors, designers), and marketing expenses. These can range from $200-$800 annually for basic setup and maintenance.
- Learning Curve: You may need to acquire new skills in areas like marketing, distribution, and financial management to ensure success.

Alternatives to Starting a Business

If you're unsure about starting a full-fledged business right away, here are some alternatives:

- Operate as a Sole Proprietor: You can sell your book under your name without formally registering a business. This is simpler but lacks the legal protections of an LLC.

- *Focus on Marketing Your Book First: Before committing to a business structure, test the waters by promoting your book through social media, local events, or online platforms like Amazon KDP. This will help you gauge interest and potential profitability.*
- *Collaborate with Freelancers: Instead of building a team or hiring full-time staff, work with freelance editors, designers, and marketers to keep costs manageable while maintaining quality.*

When Starting a Business Makes Sense

You should consider starting a business if:

1. You plan to publish multiple books or expand into related ventures like speaking engagements, workshops, or courses.

2. You want to publish books by other authors in addition to your own work.

3. You aim to build a long-term brand around your writing or expertise.

4. You want the legal protections and tax benefits that come with forming an LLC or corporation.

Steps to Start Your Publishing Business

If you decide starting a business is the right

move, here are the steps:

1. Define Your Goals: Clarify what you want to achieve with your publishing business— whether it's selling more books, building authority in your field, or creating additional revenue streams.

2. Choose a Business Structure: Decide between operating as an LLC (recommended for liability protection) or another structure based on your needs.

3. Register Your Business: Obtain necessary permits and an Employer Identification Number (EIN) for tax purposes.

4. Set Up Infrastructure: Create a professional website, set up accounting systems, and secure ISBNs for your books.

5. Develop Marketing Strategies: Plan how you'll promote your book(s) through social media ads, email campaigns, book reviews, and events.

Final Advice

Starting a business can be rewarding but requires careful planning. If you're committed to building a long-term career as an author or entrepreneur in the publishing world, forming a company may be worth it. However, if you're primarily focused on promoting one book for now, consider testing its success before taking *on the additional responsibilities of running a business.*

Evaluate your goals carefully and start small if needed—success in self-publishing often builds over time!

Well, that's a long response, but the query touched on a complicated issue.

Start a publishing company?

If you plan to have a writing career to publish more than one or two books, then you may want to consider establishing a publishing company.

I see two potential queries here. The first is similar to the query in the previous section: I just self-published my first book. I'm wondering if I should start a business. What do you advise?

The second query considers a broader view of a business.

Query

I'm considering starting a publishing business that will accept books from other authors. How do you recommend I go about doing this?

Response

Starting a publishing business that accepts books from other authors is an exciting venture that involves several key steps. Here's a comprehensive guide to help you get started:

1. Define Your Business Goals and Vision

- *Set Clear Objectives: Determine what types of books you want to publish and your target audience. Decide whether you will publish only certain genres or a wide range of literary works.*
- *Create a Business Plan: Outline your mission, long-term and short-term goals, strategies for achieving these goals, and financial projections. This plan will serve as your roadmap and should be revisited periodically to adapt to changes.*

2. Legal and Structural Setup

- *Choose a Business Structure: Decide whether to establish your company as a sole proprietorship, partnership, or limited liability company (LLC). An LLC is often recommended because it offers liability protection.*
- *Register Your Business: Obtain necessary permits and register with the appropriate*

government authorities. In the U.S., this includes obtaining an Employer Identification Number (EIN) from the IRS.

3. Build Your Brand

- *Create a Brand Identity: Develop a unique name and logo for your publishing imprint. This brand will represent your company on all published books and marketing materials.*
- *Establish an Online Presence: Set up a professional website and social media profiles to promote your company and attract authors.*

4. Develop Infrastructure

- *Set Up Operations: Establish administrative systems such as accounting software, a business bank account, and methods for managing book production (e.g., print-on-demand).*
- *Build a Team: Initially, you might hire freelancers for tasks like editing, cover design, and marketing. As your business grows, consider hiring full-time staff.*

5. Acquire Manuscripts

- *Submission Process: Define how authors can submit their manuscripts to you. This could involve setting guidelines for submissions and creating a system to evaluate potential projects.*

- *Select Manuscripts: Choose works that align with your publishing goals and have market potential. Consider factors like literary quality and genre trends.*

6. Publish and Market Books

- *Production: Once you've selected manuscripts, focus on editing, designing covers, and formatting the books for print or digital distribution.*
- *Marketing Strategy: Develop marketing plans tailored to each book's target audience. Use social media, book promotion websites, and possibly paid advertising to reach readers.*

7. Financial Management

- *Budgeting: Create a detailed budget covering startup costs, ongoing expenses, and revenue projections. Consider costs such as registration fees, marketing expenses, and personnel salaries.*
- *Funding Options: Explore various funding options like self-funding, seeking investors, or crowdfunding to support your business operations.*

By following these steps, you can establish a successful publishing company that attracts talented authors and produces engaging books for readers. Remember that the publishing industry is competitive, so continuous learning and adaptation are crucial to staying relevant in the market.

Overall, this is an excellent startup plan. An alternative to accepting other authors is to start a publishing company exclusively for your own books. That's what I did when I started Strange Worlds Publishing.

Master Query List

This section provides a list of AI queries used in the book. You can copy and use them as is or you can modify them to suit your own situation.

General queries

General query: What {issues/habits/ whatever} should writers avoid?

Research query: How can writers and authors use AI for research on {insert topic}?

Research query: Show me a list of websites that have information on {topic}.

Outline query: Provide an outline for the {book/research paper/website}{insert description}.

Brainstorming query: Brainstorm the following {insert topic}.

Brainstorming query: I have this idea

about {enter idea description}. Expand the idea by brainstorming possible {applications/ expansions/whatever}.

Getting help query: How can a writer utilize AI to support their writing projects?

Youtube video query: Write a 300-word summary for this video {insert Youtube link}.

Phase 1: Planning queries

Character query: What traits should a writer try to develop in a character like {character name}?

Character query: What makes {character name} a great character?

Plot query: I want to write a story that involves {storyline or description}. Develop a plot for this story.

Writer's block query: I'm stuck on my [genre} story. Give me a list of ideas on {character development/plot/themes/settings/ whatever}.

Outline query: I plan to write a nonfiction book called {title} that will {description}. Generate an outline for the book. The book is nonfiction and doesn't require characters or a plot.

Character query: What traits should a writer try to develop in a character?

Optional plot query: Analyze the plot of {enter story title}.

Phase 2: Writing queries

Query: What should fiction writers avoid doing while writing the first draft?

Title query: My new fiction story is {genre} and here is the {synopsis or storyline}. Generate a list of appropriate titles for the story.

Editing query: Edit the following piece and highlight your changes: {paste text here}.

Editing and SDT query: Edit the following piece, highlight your changes and point out examples where show-don't-tell can be used {paste text here}

Rewrite query: Rewrite this {insert text} two different ways: one in a light-hearted tone, one in a pompous tone:

Stuck Query: My character is {describe situation}. Tell me {number} ways he {describe solution}.

Phase 3: Publishing queries

Fiction query: My {title} is a {genre} book about {brief description}. Write a query letter targeted at an agent.

Nonfiction query: My {title} is a nonfiction book about {brief description}. Write a query letter targeted at an agent.

Query: What do self-publishing authors often do wrong?

Keywords query: {book description or storyline} Generate a set of relevant keywords.

Book blurb query (book description or storyline}. Create a 50-word book blurb and insert keywords where appropriate.

Book description query: {insert text} Write a {length} description using keywords where possible.

Category query: {insert description} What book categories should I use with Kindle?

Optional query: List the keywords for {enter title of book}.

Phase 4: Marketing queries

Marketing query: My new book will be launched in a few weeks. How do I market it?

Strategic marketing query: Why is a strategic marketing plan so important for book marketing?

Fiction novel strategic marketing query: Develop a strategic marketing plan for my humorous fantasy novel.

Nonfiction book strategic marketing query: Develop a strategic marketing plan for my new nonfiction book on how writers can utilize AI programs.

Hashtags query: {insert storyline} Generate list of appropriate hashtags

Press release query: {insert storyline} Write a press release using keywords where possible.

Book launch marketing plan: My new book will be launched on {insert date}. Prepare a six week launch marketing plan for this launch event starting two weeks before launch.

Targeting query: How can I reach my targeted audience for {insert genre}?

Targeting query: My novel is a {insert genre} story. How can I reach {inter genre} readers rather than the general population?

Social media posts: {Insert storyline} write 5 social media posts for {insert social media platform}

Blog posts: {insert storyline} write {insert length} blog post using keywords.

Trailers: {insert description} create the script for a seven {or other number} slide trailer

Optional query: Write 5 satiric Facebook posts on {enter subject}.

Phase 5: Author business queries

General business query: What do new authors overlook when it comes to business {or other issues}?

Breaking even: How will I know when my book royalties will equal or exceed my expenses?

Business problem: I'm having trouble with {insert issue}. Provide a detailed list of ways to {fix/solve/eliminate} this issue with details.

Starting a publishing company: I'm considering starting a publishing business that will accept books from other authors. How do you recommend I go about doing this?

About the Author

Hank Quense writes humorous and satiric sci-fi and fantasy stories. He also writes and lectures about fiction writing, self-publishing, book marketing and author business. He has published 21 books and 50 short stories along with dozens of articles.

His two daughters and five grandchildren live in nearby towns.

Other books by Hank Quense
The books are arranged by series on webpages called Padlets. Click on the link to see the Padlet (I love Padlets!)
Fiction:
https://padlet.com/hanque/fiction-fkoyyhe0zbprq8u2
Non-fiction:
https://padlet.com/hanque/non-fiction-resources-u31nc6aa8wpz4hcw
You can find all these books on Amazon and other book sellers

Freebies:
https://padlet.com/hanque/free-books-gpdxh7hm98pyj1x9

Links? you want links?

Website: https://hankquense.com

Newsletter sign up: https://hankquense.substack.com/subscribe

Twitter: https://x.com/hanque99

YouTube: https://www.youtube.com/@CreatingANovel-n9i

Facebook: https://www.facebook.com/hank.quense

Instagram: https://www.instagram.com/hquense/

Goodreads: https://www.goodreads.com/author/show/3002079.Hank_Quense